Learn
Microsoft®
Windows® Me
Millenium Edition

Send Us Your Comments:

To comment on this book or any other PRIMA TECH title, visit PRIMA TECH's reader response page on the Web at http://www.prima-tech.com/comments.

How to Order:

For information on quantity discounts, contact the publisher: Prima Publishing, P.O. Box 1260BK, Rocklin, CA 95677-1260; (916) 787-7000. On your letterhead, include information concerning the intended use of the books and the number of books you wish to purchase. For individual orders, visit PRIMA TECH's Web site at http://www.prima-tech.com.

Learn
Microsoft®
Windows® Me
Millenium Edition

A Division of Prima Publishing

LOIS LOWE

A Division of Prima Publishing

Prima Publishing and colophon are registered trademarks of Prima Communications, Inc. PRIMA TECH is a trademark of Prima Communications, Inc., Roseville, California 95661.

Microsoft, Windows, and Internet Explorer are trademarks or registered trademarks of Microsoft Corporation. Mac and Macintosh are trademarks or registered trademarks of Apple Computer, Inc. Netscape is a registered trademark of Netscape Communications Corporation.

Important: Prima Publishing cannot provide software support. Please contact the appropriate software manufacturer's technical support line or Web site for assistance.

Prima Publishing and the authors have attempted throughout this book to distinguish proprietary trademarks from descriptive terms by following the capitalization style used by the manufacturers.

Information contained in this book has been obtained by Prima Publishing from sources believed to be reliable. However, because of the possibility of human or mechanical error by our sources, Prima Publishing, or others, the Publisher does not guarantee the accuracy, adequacy, or completeness of any information and is not responsible for any errors or omissions or the results obtained from the use of such information. Readers should be particularly aware of the fact that the Internet is an ever-changing entity. Some facts might have changed since this book went to press.

ISBN: 0-7615-3297-8

Library of Congress Catalog Card Number: 0010906

Printed in the United States of America

00 01 02 03 04 DD 10 9 8 7 6 5 4 3 2 1

Publisher:
Stacy L. Hiquet

Marketing Manager:
Judi Taylor

Associate Marketing Manager:
Jody Kennen

Managing Editor:
Sandy Doell

Acquisitions Editor:
Lynette Quinn

Project Editor:
Melody Layne

Copy Editor:
Kezia Endsley

Technical Reviewer:
Dennis Teague

Proofreader:
Jessica McCarty

Interior Layout:
Danielle Foster

Cover Design:
Prima Design Team

Indexer:
Sharon Shock

In memory of Lois Adams Lowe, a true one-of-a-kind original

ACKNOWLEDGEMENTS

Thanks to the great editorial staff at Prima Publishing for all their hard work in publishing this book, including Lynette Quinn, Melody Layne, Kezia Endsley, and Dennis Teague. Thanks also to M.A.C., my lifeline, and my family, and to Joan and Linda for all the fine garden produce this summer and especially the blackberries!

CONTENTS AT A GLANCE

CONTENTS

SATURDAY MORNING
Exploring the Windows Accessories 35

SATURDAY AFTERNOON
Customizing Your System

SATURDAY EVENING
Improving System Performance 161

SUNDAY MORNING

INTRODUCTION

Almost anyone who owns a Windows-based computer wishes he or she knew more about it. Perhaps you wish you knew how to remove some of the programs that came with your PC that you never use, or how to troubleshoot a puzzling error message. Or maybe you just want to put the screen colors back the way they were before your 12-year-old nephew got a hold of it.

Learn Microsoft Windows Me in a Weekend can save you lots of time and frustration. It's a deluxe tour of Windows Me, starting with the basics and moving on up to the tricky parts. Along the way, you'll learn about file and program management, customizing your system, keeping your hard disk in good working order, and using some of the latest and greatest multimedia features such as Media Player and Movie Maker. Even if you're not all that technically oriented, I promise it'll be fun.

How to Use This Book

This book is divided into seven sessions. You can do them in chronological order or skip around—whatever works best for you.

○ **Friday Evening: No Experience Required**. This first session explains basic Windows operation, including how to run programs, manage files, and install or remove software.

✪ **Saturday Morning: Exploring the Windows Accessories**. Here you take a tour through the accessory programs that come free with Windows, including the new Windows Media Player and Windows Movie Maker. You'll also learn about acquiring graphics from a scanner or digital camera.

✪ **Saturday Afternoon: Customizing Your System.** This is the place to learn about changing screen colors, system sounds, mouse pointers, and all those other nifty little tweaks that make the system your own.

✪ **Saturday Evening: Improving System Performance.** Windows comes with a variety of utilities that can help make your system run better, and in this session you'll try them out.

✪ **Sunday Morning: Exploring the Internet**. This session shows you how to set up an Internet connection, how to use Internet Explorer to surf the Web, and how to receive and send e-mail and newsgroup messages with Outlook Express.

✪ **Sunday Afternoon: More Fun Things to Try**. This session includes a hodge-podge of interesting intermediate-level activities for the curious users wanting to go further with Windows. Here you'll learn about home networking, user profiles, working with DVD and CD-RW, and lots more.

✪ **Appendix A: Troubleshooting Problems.** If you are having problems with your system, this appendix is the place to turn. It provides detailed step-by-step help for troubleshooting problems with Windows itself, with devices, and with individual programs.

Special Features of This Book

Several special elements in this book will help you on your way.

TIP Tips offer insider information about a technology, a company, or a technique.

NOTE   Notes provide background information and insight into why things work the way they do.

CAUTION   Cautions warn you of possible hazards and point out pitfalls that typically plague beginners.

No Experience Required

- ✿ Introducing Windows
- ✿ Working with a Window
- ✿ Using Menus, Toolbars, and Dialog Boxes
- ✿ Working with Files
- ✿ Working with Programs

f you're a beginner using a Windows-based computer, this chapter is for you. It contains all the basic information you need to know in order to keep up with the rest of the weekend's sessions.

Are you upgrading from Windows 95/98, or already using Windows Millennium at home or work? If so, much of this session will be a review. You can skip it entirely, or skim through to fill in the gaps in your previous education.

Introducing Windows

Microsoft Windows is an operating system for personal computers. An *operating system* handles the mundane behind-the-scenes tasks that the computer needs to operate, and acts as a communication interface between the user (that's you!) and the processor (the computer's "brain").

Windows has a *graphical user interface* (GUI), which means it uses both pictures and text to help you communicate with the processor. You use a pointer onscreen to issue commands. In contrast, MS-DOS, the original PC operating system, was text-only, and you issued commands by typing. Figure 1.1 shows a typical Windows screen.

The latest consumer version of Windows is Windows Millennium Edition, or Me. It replaces Windows 98, which in turn replaced Windows 95. There are other versions of Windows out there too, such as Windows 2000, designed for corporate use. Windows 2000 replaced Windows NT 4, the earlier corporate version.

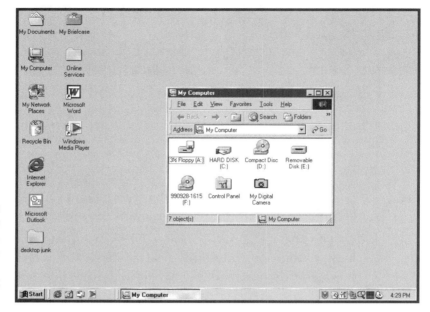

Figure 1.1

Windows is a graphical interface, using a combination of pictures and text to interact with users.

This book is about Windows Me, but because all versions of Windows are similar, this book can help you master the basics of almost any Windows version. When you read later in the book about specific utilities and accessories, however, note that other versions of Windows might not include the same ones.

Starting Up and Shutting Down

To start up a PC with Windows installed on it, simply turn the PC on by pressing its Power button. Windows loads automatically. It takes about 1–2 minutes for it to load up from a cold start, and as it loads, you'll see various bits of information appear and disappear, such as the name of the video card and the amount of memory installed. If you don't see anything onscreen, make sure the monitor is turned on. See Appendix A for troubleshooting help if needed.

You should not shut down a Windows PC by pressing the Power button, however, because Windows might be in the middle of doing something important. Shutting down a PC abruptly like that can result in disk errors. (You'll learn how to correct them on Saturday Evening.)

Instead, you should use the Shut Down command in Windows. Here's how:

1. Use the mouse to point to the Start button in the bottom-left corner of the screen.

2. Press and release the left mouse button. A menu appears.

    Pressing and releasing the left mouse button is called *clicking*. In the rest of this book, I'll simply tell you to *click* this or that button or picture onscreen.

NOTE Click: To press and release the left mouse button once while the mouse pointer is pointing at a certain button, command, or option onscreen.

3. Click the Shut Down command on the menu. A dialog box appears.

4. Click the down-pointing arrow in the box. A menu drops down.

5. Click Shut Down on that menu. Shut Down appears in the text box to the left of the arrow you clicked. See Figure 1.2.

6. Click the OK button.

At this point, one of two things happens. Either the PC shuts itself off, or a message appears onscreen telling you that it is now safe for you to shut off your computer. If you see that message, press the PC's Power button to turn it off.

You don't have to shut down the computer every time you walk away from it. Some people leave theirs on all the time. You might want to shut it

Figure 1.2

Use the Shut Down Windows dialog box to properly shut down your computer each time.

down during a lightning storm or when you'll be away on vacation, but other than that you can safely leave it on. Windows contains power management features that will automatically turn off the monitor after a certain period of inactivity, but it turns back on again when you press a key or move the mouse.

Getting Around Onscreen

Take a moment to familiarize yourself with these parts of the Windows display, pointed out in Figure 1.3.

⚙ **Desktop.** The colored background that everything else sits on.

⚙ **Icons.** The little pictures with words beneath them. Each icon represents a program, a data file, or a shortcut for performing some activity.

⚙ **Mouse pointer.** The arrow that moves onscreen when you move your mouse.

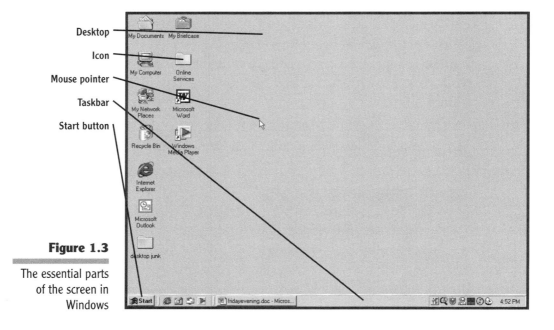

Figure 1.3

The essential parts of the screen in Windows

- ⚙ **Taskbar.** The bar at the bottom of the screen containing a clock and several small icons.

- ⚙ **Start button.** The button at the bottom-left corner of the screen. Clicking it opens the menu system.

Icons and Shortcuts

Each of the little pictures on the desktop is an *icon* and represents some sort of program, utility, or data file. To activate an icon, you double-click on it— that is, press and release the left mouse button twice quickly. Activating the icon can mean different things depending on what the icon represents. For example, in Figure 1.4, I double-clicked the My Computer icon and the My Computer window opened up (which contains—you guessed it—more icons). If I double-clicked on an icon of one of my word processing files, the document would open in my word processor for editing.

NOTE Double-click: To press and release the left mouse button twice quickly in succession.

I double-clicked
on this icon...

...to open this window

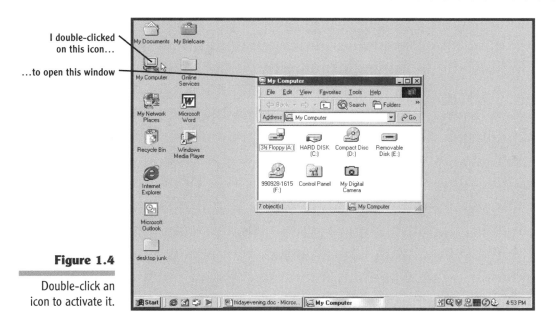

Figure 1.4

Double-click an
icon to activate it.

In Windows, almost everything shows up as an icon—drives, folders, documents, programs, and so on. Some icons correspond to actual files on your hard disk, so that deleting the icon deletes the file; other icons are merely *shortcuts* to the actual files, and deleting the shortcut does nothing to the file it refers to. That distinction will be important later, when you start moving and deleting files, but for now just shove the fact to the back of your mind.

The Start Menu

As you saw earlier in the chapter, clicking the Start button opens the Start menu. This menu is your gateway to running programs, using utilities to change your system settings, controlling devices such as printers, and more.

When you open the Start menu, you might see a few select programs listed at the very top, but the majority of the installed programs are in submenus. To see a submenu, point at any of the words on the Start menu with right-pointing triangles next to them, and a submenu flies out from it. You can then click the command on the submenu you want, or display another layer of submenus. See Figure 1.5.

Figure 1.5

The Start button provides an entry to the menu system.

Windows Me includes a *personalized menus* feature that customizes the Start menu to show the commands you use most often first. If you see a double-arrow pointing down at the bottom of a menu or submenu, it means that this feature is enabled, and not all the menu's commands appear. To see the rest of them, click that double-arrow to expand the menu. Every time you choose a command, Windows remembers, and the next time you open that menu, that command appears on the "short list" that comes up right away. Figure 1.6 shows the adaptive menus feature in use. Notice that the Programs menu is still compressed, and there's a double-headed down arrow at the bottom. The Accessories menu is expanded; some of the commands look "pressed in," indicating they were not on the short list.

Figure 1.6

The Start menu with the personalized menus feature active

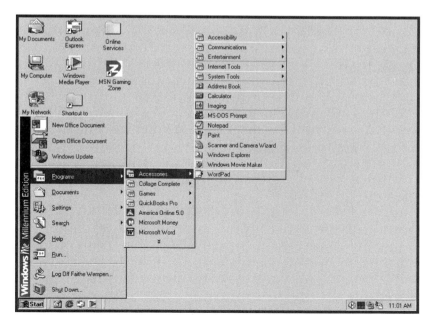

NOTE The personalized menus feature is enabled by default in new installations of Windows Me; if you upgrade from a previous version, it's disabled by default.

Some people find these personalized menus helpful; to other people they're annoying. If you want to turn them off, do the following:

1. Right-click the taskbar and choose Properties.

NOTE Right-click: To press and release the right mouse button once. Right-clicking opens a shortcut menu. You'll learn more about shortcut menus later in the chapter.

2. Deselect the Use Personalized Menus check box.

3. Click OK.

In this book, I show personalized menus turned off, because everyone's screen looks different with the feature on based on what commands they have been using. Turning this feature off in the figures I show you in this book helps eliminate that confusion.

The Taskbar

The taskbar is the gray bar at the bottom of the screen. When a window is open, a rectangular bar appears on the taskbar corresponding to it. You can have many windows open at once, containing a variety of content: file listings, programs, and so on, but only one window can be active at a time. The active window appears with a different colored title bar (the bar across its top), and its button appears "pressed in" on the taskbar. To choose which window is active, click anywhere within the window or click its button on the taskbar. Figure 1.7 shows two windows open.

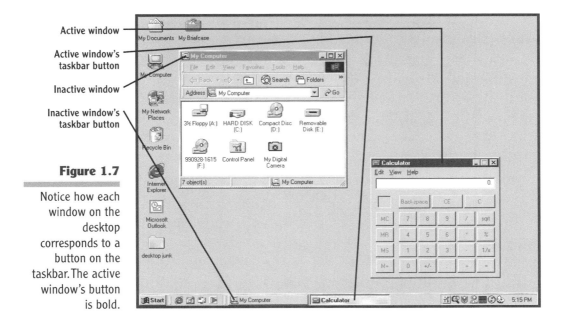

Active window

Active window's taskbar button

Inactive window

Inactive window's taskbar button

Figure 1.7

Notice how each window on the desktop corresponds to a button on the taskbar. The active window's button is bold.

Working with a Window

A *window* is a rectangular-shaped box that contains a running program, a list of files, or a set of options for configuring something. (When the window contains options or settings, it's typically called a *dialog box*, because it enables you to have a dialogue with the program.) As you can guess by the name Microsoft Windows, these windows figure heavily into the total picture.

You've already seen several ways of opening a window. Double-clicking on an icon opens a window, as does selecting a command from the Start menu.

A window can have three states: *maximized, restored,* or *minimized.* A maximized window fills the entire screen, as in Figure 1.8. A restored window takes up *some* space, but not the entire screen. A minimized window doesn't appear at all; the only evidence of it is on the taskbar. Figure 1.9 shows a restored and a minimized window.

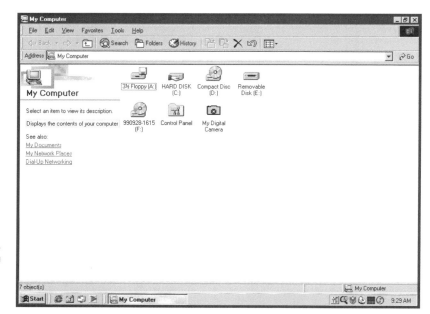

Figure 1.8

A maximized window fills the screen.

Restored window

Minimized window

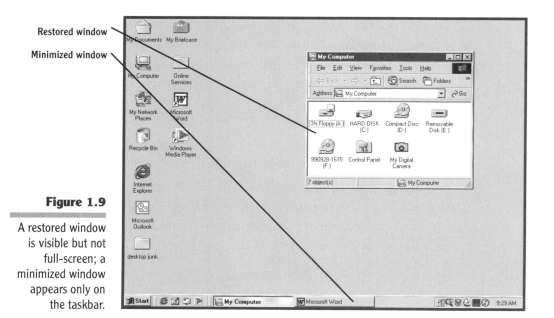

Figure 1.9

A restored window is visible but not full-screen; a minimized window appears only on the taskbar.

To control a window's state, use the buttons in its top-right corner:

Minimize

Maximize (appears only if restored)

Restore (appears only if maximized)

Close

The Close button closes the window entirely. If the window contains a program, the program shuts down and clears itself from memory.

When a window is not maximized, there's some room for it to move around onscreen. You can move a window by dragging its title bar. As you drag, you can see an outline of where the window is going, as in Figure 1.10.

NOTE   Drag: To point and click something with the mouse pointer, and then hold down the left mouse button as you move the mouse.

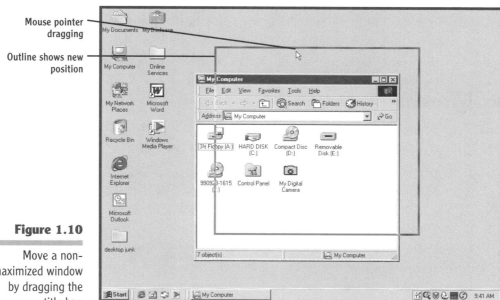

Figure 1.10

Move a non-maximized window by dragging the title bar.

Mouse pointer dragging

Outline shows new position

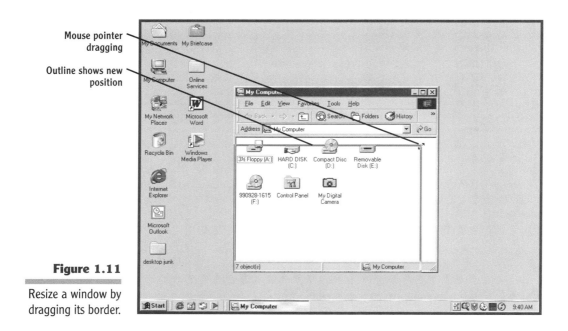

Figure 1.11

Resize a window by dragging its border.

To resize a window, drag one of its borders. You can resize in one dimension at a time by dragging a side, or resize both height and width at once by dragging a corner. Figure 1.11 shows a corner being dragged inward to make the window smaller. Notice that the outline shows the window's new size.

Using Menus

You have already seen the big menu: the Start menu. It opens when you click the Start button, and it contains a listing of programs and utilities you can run.

Most windows also have a menu system. The menu bar appears directly under the title bar and contains the names of drop-down menus. To open a menu (this is, drop it down), click the name. Then, once a menu is open, click the command you want to select from it. Figure 1.12 shows an open menu.

I clicked here to open
the Edit menu

Click a menu command
to select it

Some commands are
unavailable

Each menu name and
command has a
selection letter

Some commands have
shortcut key
combinations

Figure 1.12

Most windows have
one or more drop-
down menus.

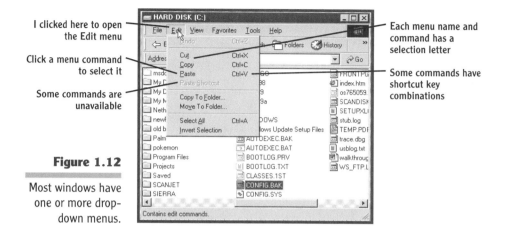

The menu in Figure 1.12 shows several important features of menus:

❖ Not all commands are available all the time. Unavailable commands appear dimmed.

❖ Some commands have shortcut key combinations you can press instead of opening the menu and choosing the command. These appear to the right of the command.

❖ Each menu name has an underlined letter, called a selection letter. You can hold down the Alt key and type the selection letter to open the menu. Each command has one too; when a menu is open you can type the selection letter of the command you want (no need to use Alt).

❖ Some commands have an ellipsis (three dots) after them. These commands open dialog boxes, prompting you for additional information.

You might occasionally run into some other types of menu features. Figure 1.13 shows some of them:

❖ Commands with a right-pointing arrow open a submenu, which includes more options within that category.

Submenu

On/off toggle

These commands work
as a group

Dividers set off
the group

Figure 1.13

Other menu
features to be
aware of

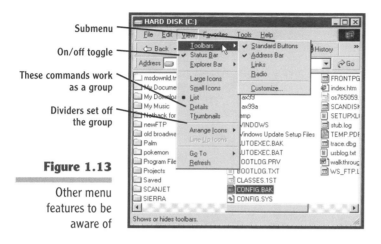

- ✦ Some commands are on/off toggles for a feature. A check mark indicates the feature is currently on.

- ✦ Some commands work as a mutually exclusive group. The chosen item has a dot beside it; when you choose a different one in the set, the former choice becomes unselected.

- ✦ Groups of commands are often set apart with a horizontal divider line.

There's one other kind of menu: a shortcut menu. Whenever you right-click an object onscreen, a shortcut menu appears for it, containing commands for the most common actions you might take. Shortcut menus have different commands on them depending on the object type. For example, Figure 1.14 shows two shortcut menus—one for an icon on the desktop and one for the taskbar.

Figure 1.14

Two shortcut
menus, each
appropriate for the
object to which it
belongs

Almost all shortcut menus contain a Properties command. You can choose it to set the properties, or options, for the clicked-upon item. You'll see later in this book how handy this is for customizing the way Windows (or a particular object) looks and acts.

Using Toolbars

Most windows contain some sort of toolbar. A *toolbar* is a row of buttons (usually graphical), typically appearing directly beneath the menu bar. Each button is a shortcut for one of the menu commands. For example, there might be a Delete button you can click instead of opening the Edit menu and choosing the Delete command. Depending on the program and its settings, a toolbar button can contain just a graphic, text and a graphic, or just text.

In most programs, you can point to (but not click) a graphical toolbar button to see a ScreenTip (a pop-up message) containing the button's name. This can help you determine what each button in a toolbar does. Figure 1.15 shows a ScreenTip for a toolbar button.

Using Dialog Boxes

As I mentioned earlier, some menu commands (namely the ones with ellipses next to them on the menus) open dialog boxes. A dialog box requests additional information from you before executing a command. For example, when you open the File menu and choose Print in some programs, a Print dialog box appears asking how many copies, what printer to use, what page range to print, and so on.

Figure 1.15

ScreenTips tell you a button's name, and from that you can deduce its purpose.

The controls in a dialog box are fairly self-explanatory. Here's a quick summary:

- **Check boxes (square).** These turn individual features on/off independently of one another.

- **Option buttons (round).** These operate in groups of mutually exclusive options. Turning one on turns another off, like on a car radio.

- **Drop-down lists.** To use these, click the down-pointing arrow next to a text box to open a list from which to choose. In some cases you must choose from the list; in others you can type your own entry in the box if nothing on the list matches your needs.

- **Command buttons.** These are rectangular buttons with text on them, such as OK or Cancel. OK closes the dialog box retaining your changes. Cancel closes it discarding your changes. Other command buttons might open other dialog boxes or expand the current dialog box.

- **Increment arrows.** These are up and down arrows next to a text box that contain a numeric value. You can increment the number up or down with the buttons.

See Figure 1.16 for a dialog box example that uses most of these elements.

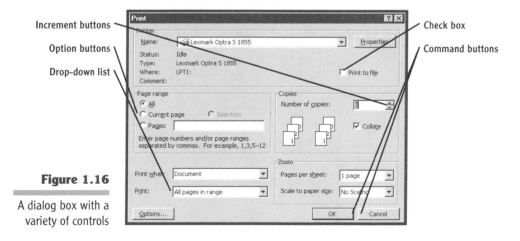

Figure 1.16

A dialog box with a variety of controls

Take a Break

Ready for a stretch break? If you are working with Windows for the very first time, this information can be pretty overwhelming all at once. You might want to take some time to just play with Windows, rather than reading about it so studiously! Then come back and learn about files and programs in the remainder of the session.

Working with Files

The whole computing concept is based on *files*. A file is a collection of data stored under a single name. Here are some examples of files:

- ✿ A word processing document that you create in an application such as Microsoft Word.

- ✿ A printer driver (a utility file that helps Windows send data to your printer).

- ✿ An application file (a file that runs a program that you use for some useful purpose, such as word processing).

- ✿ A Windows helper file such as a DLL or VXD file (behind-the-scenes files that keep Windows running).

What can you do with files? Well, some files do things all by themselves, without any direct intervention. The files that keep Windows running are like that, for example, as are the files that check your system for viruses in the background as you work.

Other files run programs. When you choose a program to run from the Start menu, the file that runs the program executes, presenting the program on your screen to work with.

Still other files hold your stored data from programs. You can move, copy, or delete such files as needed. For example, you might copy a word processing file onto a floppy disk, or delete an unwanted spreadsheet file. You'll learn how to move, copy, and delete files later in this chapter.

Files, Folders, and Disks

Files are stored on *disks*. There are many kinds of disks: hard disks, floppy disks, CD-ROMs, and so on. Each of them is read by a disk drive. The hard disk is not removable; its disk and its drive are a single unit. A floppy disk or CD-ROM, in contrast, can be inserted into or removed from your system's floppy or CD-ROM drive.

When a disk contains a lot of files, it's easy to get confused. *Folders* help avoid confusion by providing an organizational structure in which to store the files. For example, on your hard disk, there is a Windows folder that contains the files needed to run Windows, and a My Documents folder that stores the data files you create. When you install new software, it creates its own new folder on your hard disk. Most Windows programs create subfolders for themselves in the Program Files folder.

A file's location in the folder hierarchy is known as its *path*. A path starts out with the drive and then lists the first-level folder, and then the second, and so on, like this:

C:\Windows\System\drwatson.exe

In this case, the file name is drwatson.exe. It's located in a folder called System, which is in a folder called Windows, which is on the C drive.

File Names and Extensions

A file's name in Windows can be up to 256 characters, and can include spaces and symbols (except for a few off-limits symbols such as ?, *, and /).

Each file has an extension—a code that tells what type of file it is. The extension is separated from the name by a period. So, for example, if you see drwatson.exe, drwatson is the file name and .exe is the extension. The .exe extension indicates that it's an executable file, a.k.a. a program.

Earlier operating systems such as MS-DOS had an 8.3 file-naming limit. In other words, file names could be a maximum of eight characters, and extensions could be a maximum of three characters, with no spaces allowed. Even though those regulations no longer apply in Windows 95 and above, it is still customary to limit file names and extensions to 8.3 whenever possible.

● ●

NOTE If you ever have a problem with your PC, you might need to start it using an emergency boot disk, which places the PC in MS-DOS mode. When you do that, you must stick with 8.3 file names. If a file has a longer name than that, or if the name includes spaces, it becomes truncated in MS-DOS mode listings with a ~ sign and a number. So, for example, the C:\Program Files folder becomes C:\Progra~1. See Appendix A, "Troubleshooting Problems," for more system troubleshooting information.

● ●

Windows Explorer and My Computer

When you double-click the My Computer icon in the desktop, a window appears with icons for each drive on your system (plus a few additional icons that I address later). You can then double-click a drive icon to see all the files and folders stored on that drive. See Figure 1.17.

Windows Explorer is another way of looking at a drive's contents. To open Windows Explorer, click the Start button, point to Programs, point to Accessories, and then click Windows Explorer.

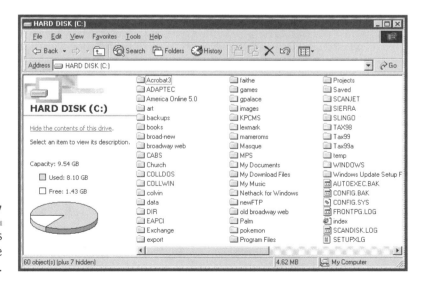

Figure 1.17

My Computer shows a single-pane file listing.

Toggle the folder tree pane on/off with this button

Folder tree

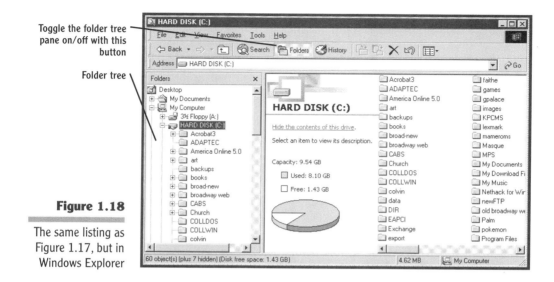

Figure 1.18

The same listing as Figure 1.17, but in Windows Explorer

Windows Explorer has two panes. The right pane is just like My Computer; the left pane is a folder *tree*, a hierarchical representation of the folders and drives available on your PC. See Figure 1.18.

My Computer and Windows Explorer are not really different programs; they're simply different views of the same program. To prove this, click the Folders button on the toolbar in either one, thus toggling the display of the folder listing (the left pane). Turn the folder listing on in My Computer, and it becomes Windows Explorer.

In the folder listing, plus signs appear next to folders that have subfolders not displayed on the tree at the moment. Minus signs appear next to folders whose complete subfolder structure is displayed.

Also on your desktop, you'll find icons that open file-management windows for two commonly used locations: the My Documents folder (the default location for data files) and My Network Places. These folders are also accessible through the folder tree in Windows Explorer; the icons on the desktop are merely alternative, quick ways of accessing them.

Selecting Files

When working with files and folders, you first select the file (or files) you want to affect, and then you issue a command to affect them. That command can be Move, Copy, Delete, Rename, or some other activity.

To select a file or folder, click on it once. A selected file appears highlighted. To select more than one file or folder at once, hold down Ctrl as you click on each item you want to include in the grouping. You can select a whole series of adjacent files by clicking the first one, and then holding down Shift as you click on the last one. Figure 1.19 shows several files and folders selected.

NOTE

When you select a folder, you affect every file contained within that folder by your next command. For example, deleting a folder deletes all the files within it.

Selected files

List of the selected files

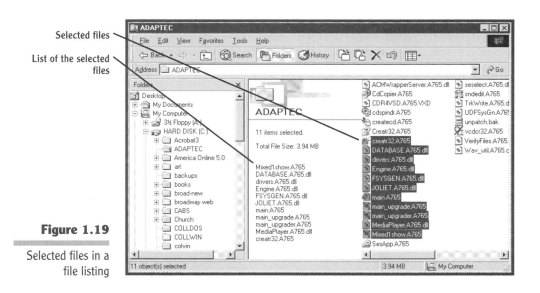

Figure 1.19

Selected files in a file listing

Moving and Copying Files

Once you have selected one or more files, you can move or copy them. You might copy a word processing file to a floppy disk to give to a coworker, for example, or move files that you seldom use to another drive for storage.

◆ ◆

CAUTION The only files you should move are files you have created yourself. If you move files that belong to a certain program or to Windows itself, they might not be able to perform their duties anymore.

◆ ◆

You can move and copy files in several ways. Pick whichever works best for you:

✪ You can drag-and-drop files. To do so, click and drag the selected files to a different drive or folder. Hold down Ctrl to copy or Shift during the dragging to move. Make sure the Folders pane is displayed so you can see the destination before you start dragging.

● ●

NOTE Drag-and-drop: To move or copy something by dragging it where you want it and dropping it there (by releasing the mouse button).

● ●

✪ You can use the Copy or Cut commands on the Edit menu to place the files on the Clipboard, a temporary holding area, display the desired destination, and then use the Paste command on the Edit menu to paste the files there.

✪ You can use the Copy To or Move To buttons on the toolbar. Clicking on one opens a Browse for Folder window, shown in Figure 1.20. Use it to select the destination for the file(s) and click on OK.

Creating New Folders

Notice in Figure 1.20, there's a New Folder button. You can use that as you are moving or copying to graft a new branch onto the folder structure for a drive.

Click here to create a new folder on-the-fly

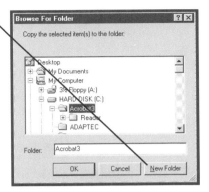

Figure 1.20

The Copy To and Move To buttons provide a box from which to choose the destination.

You can also create a new folder anytime. To do so:

1. Display the contents of the folder into which you want to put it.

   To place a new folder directly on a drive (that is, at the top level of organization), display that drive's contents.

2. Choose File, New, Folder. (In other words, open the File menu, point to New, and click Folder.)

   A new folder appears, with the name New Folder.

3. Type a new name and press Enter.

Renaming Files and Folders

To rename a file or folder, select it and press F2. Then retype the name and press Enter. Easy enough, eh? You can also select the file and then choose File, Rename, or right-click the file or folder and choose Rename from the shortcut menu. You can rename only one file or folder at a time; it doesn't work when multiple files are selected.

Deleting Files and Working with the Recycle Bin

You should not delete any files unless a) you created them yourself, or b) you are sure that they aren't needed to run any of your programs. It's way too easy for a beginner to get carried away deleting files and screw up his or her system.

That said, here's how to do it. To delete a file, select it, and then do any of the following:

- Press the Delete key.
- Right-click the file and choose Delete from the shortcut menu.
- Click the Delete button on the toolbar.
- Drag the file to the Recycle Bin icon on the desktop.

If you see a confirmation message, click the Yes button.

Deleting a file or folder does not immediately remove it from your system; instead it moves it to a special hidden folder called the Recycle Bin, which is sort of like a trash can. You can fish it back out of the Recycle Bin if you change your mind about the deletion.

CAUTION When your hard disk gets full, the Recycle Bin starts deleting the oldest files, so don't use the Recycle Bin as temporary storage for files that you can't decide about keeping. They might be gone before you make up your mind.

To view the contents of the Recycle Bin, double-click its icon on the desktop. The Recycle Bin window that opens looks a lot like a regular file-management window, as you can see in Figure 1.21.

To restore a file to its original location, select it and then choose File, Restore. To restore *all* the files, select none of them and click the Restore All button (to the left of the listing), or select them all and use File, Restore.

To empty the Recycle Bin, permanently deleting the files within it, click the Empty Recycle Bin button to the left of the listing or choose File, Empty Recycle Bin.

TIP You don't have to open the Recycle Bin to empty it. Right-click the Recycle Bin and choose Empty Recycle Bin from the shortcut menu.

Deleted files

Click here to destroy them all

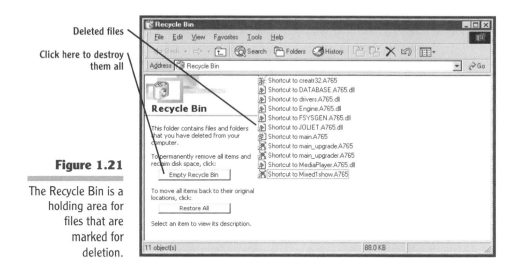

Figure 1.21

The Recycle Bin is a holding area for files that are marked for deletion.

Working with Programs

Managing files is useful, but it's not the main reason you use Windows. No, the main reason Windows exists is to run programs such as word processors, spreadsheets, games, and Internet applications.

I told you about file management first because I wanted you to understand about the different kinds of files: program files, program helper files, Windows files, and data files. When you run a program, you execute a program file. When you save your work in that program, you create a data file.

Starting and Exiting Programs

The easiest way to start a program is to select it from the Start menu. You've already seen how the Start menu operates, but here's the full-blown procedure:

1. Click the Start button.

2. Point to Programs. A list of programs appears. The list contains a combination of programs and folders. Pointing to a folder opens a submenu.

3. If you don't see the program you want to run, point to a submenu to open it.

4. When the program you want to run appears, click it.

To exit a program, click its Close (X) button in the top-right corner, or choose File, Exit. Closing a program window is the same as closing any other window. The only difference is if you've entered or changed any data, you might be prompted to save your changes. (See the following section to learn about that.)

To practice, open the WordPad program. To do so, choose Start, Programs, Accessories, WordPad. Then close the WordPad window by clicking its Close (X) button in the top-right corner.

There are other ways to start a program too. You can double-click an icon on your desktop that refers to the program, or you can double-click the executable file (.exe extension) in a file listing. But stick with the Start button method for now if you're a beginner. In the Saturday Afternoon session, I tell you about placing shortcut icons to your favorite programs on the desktop.

Finding Your Way Around in a New Program

Most Windows programs operate using some common conventions, so once you know the basics, you can find your way around in any program. For example, most programs have a File menu that contains an Exit command, allowing you to exit from the program when you're finished with it. Most File menus also include Print and Save commands.

To find out about the specifics of a new program, open the Help menu and choose a command from it to open the documentation for the program. The exact command varies among programs; in most of the Windows accessory programs it's called Help Topics. Figure 1.22 shows the Help window for the WordPad program, for example.

Windows itself has a Help system too, which you can get to using Start, Help. Once inside, browse by clicking on the underlined text hyperlinks for the topics that interest you, or search for a particular keyword or phrase in the Search box. See Figure 1.23.

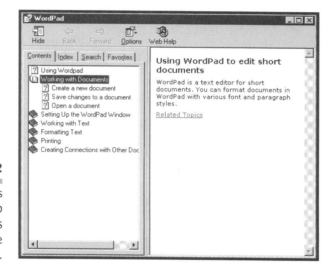

Figure 1.22

Most programs have a Help window that is accessible from the Help menu.

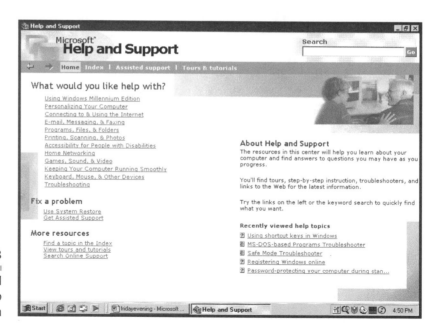

Figure 1.23

The overall Windows help system

Controlling Program Settings

You can control how some programs operate by adjusting their options or properties. Depending on the program, you might be able to set these options without starting the program, or you might need to open the program first.

Look at an example: the Recycle Bin. You can change the Recycle Bin's settings, specifying how many files are retained and for how long. To do so:

1. Right-click the Recycle Bin icon on the desktop. A shortcut menu opens.

2. Choose Properties. The Recycle Bin Properties dialog box opens. See Figure 1.24.

3. Make your selections in the dialog box to control how the Recycle Bin operates.

4. Click OK.

Right-click to open the shortcut menu

Choose Properties

The Recycle Bin Properties dialog box opens

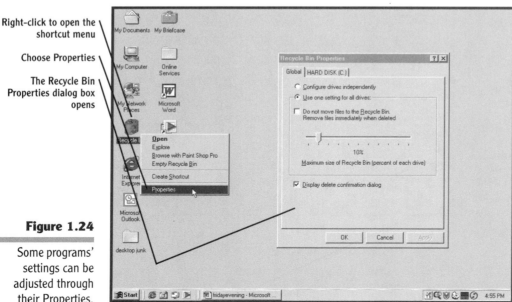

Figure 1.24

Some programs' settings can be adjusted through their Properties.

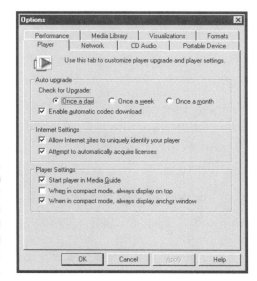

Figure 1.25

Media Player is an example of a program whose settings are adjusted from within the program.

◆ ◆

CAUTION Some of the icons on the desktop are shortcuts to other files elsewhere on your hard disk. If you set the properties for a shortcut, it doesn't affect the properties of the program to which the shortcut refers. A little arrow in the lower-left corner of the icon indicates a shortcut in most cases (see the Microsoft Word icon in Figure 1.24 for an example).

◆ ◆

With other programs, there is an Options or Settings command inside the program. For example, in Windows Media Player, you choose Tools, Options inside the program to open the Options for the player. See Figure 1.25.

Installing a New Program

When you get a new program, it probably comes on a CD. Just pop the CD into your CD-ROM drive, and the setup program will start automatically in most cases. Then follow the prompts to install the program. If the program doesn't start automatically, do the following:

1. Choose Start, Settings, Control Panel, or double-click the Control Panel icon in My Computer.

By default, Windows displays a simplified version of the Control Panel. If you see lots of icons in several rows, you are seeing the full Control Panel; if you see a list of about seven categories with underlined names, you're seeing the abbreviated one.

2. If you see the full Control Panel, double-click the Add/Remove Programs icon. Or, if you see the simplified Control Panel, click the Add/Remove Programs underlined text.

   Either way, the Add/Remove Programs Properties dialog box opens.

3. Click the Install button. See Figure 1.26.

4. Follow the prompts to find and install the setup program on the CD.

If the program doesn't start automatically, it might be because the CD-ROM drive is not set up to automatically detect a new disc insertion. See the section entitled "Setting CD Auto Insert Notification" in the Saturday Afternoon session to change that setting.

Double-click Add/Remove Programs to open this box

Click here to find a new program's setup

Remove existing programs here

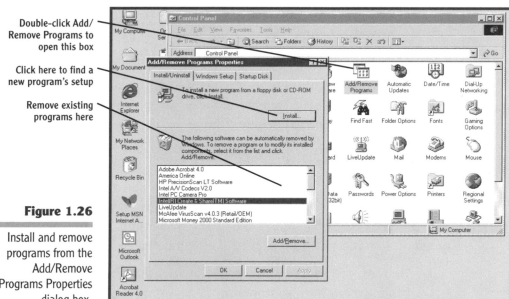

Figure 1.26

Install and remove programs from the Add/Remove Programs Properties dialog box.

Removing a Program

If there are programs on your system that you never use—perhaps programs that came with the PC or programs you've grown tired of—you can remove them to save hard disk space. Here's how:

1. Choose Start, Settings, Control Panel, or double-click the Control Panel icon in My Computer.

2. Double-click the Add/Remove Programs icon.

3. On the Install/Uninstall tab, locate the program on the list of installed programs, and click it. See Figure 1.26.

4. Click the Add/Remove button.

5. Follow the prompts to remove the program.

As you are removing the program, you might be asked about removing specific shared files. If you have any doubt, keep the file on your system. It won't hurt anything; however, if you remove a file that another program needs to operate, you can seriously mess up the other program's operation.

Controlling Which Program Opens a File Type

When you double-click on a data file, the file opens in the program that's associated with its file extension. Windows has a default set of file associations, but when you install new programs, they sometimes get changed.

For example, on a PC that does not have Microsoft Word installed, when you double-click on a file with a .doc extension, the file opens in WordPad. However, when you install Word, the setup program changes the file association for the .doc extension so that when you double-click a .doc file, it opens in Word instead of WordPad.

If you don't like the association for a particular file type, you can change it. Here's how:

1. In My Computer or Windows Explorer, locate a data file of the type that you want to change the association for.

2. Right-click the file and choose Properties. The Properties dialog box for that file appears.

Figure 1.27

Select the program
that should open
this type of file from
now on.

3. On the General tab, click the Change button. An Open With dialog box appears. See Figure 1.27.

4. Select a different program to associate with that file type. The change automatically affects all files with the same extension as the chosen file.

5. Click OK.

6. Click OK again.

I had to do this once, for example, when I installed the setup software for a new scanner I bought. It came with a graphics editing program, and that program rudely changed all the file associations for various graphics types so that they all opened by default with that program. I changed them all back to my favorite graphics editing program instead.

Wrapping Up

Now that you're up on the basics of Windows Millennium Edition, you're ready to do something useful with it! In tomorrow morning's session, I introduce you to some of the most interesting (and fun) programs that come with Windows.

Exploring the Windows Accessories

Windows comes with a whole slew of free accessory programs you can experiment with. Some of them are pretty basic, such as the calculator, whereas others are full-featured programs—as good as ones that you buy separately in stores.

I won't bore you by going over every single one of them in this book, but I do want to point out some of the ones I've found most useful, such as WordPad and Windows Media Player. So in this morning's session, prepare to play around with some fun programs.

This chapter has two main goals. One of them is to ease you further into Windows by showing you how to get around in various programs, and how to save, open, and print your work. The other is just to have some fun. Toward that end, I'll be covering what I consider to be the fun accessory programs in detail, including the two most important new programs in Windows Me: Windows Media Player and Windows Movie Maker.

Adding and Removing Accessories

Not all the Windows accessories are installed by default when you install Windows on a PC. A PC with Windows Millennium Edition preinstalled comes with a standard set of common accessories loaded, but you can add or remove accessories as desired to get the exact set you want.

To add or remove an accessory program that comes with Windows, follow these steps:

1. Choose Start, Settings, Control Panel, or double-click the Control Panel icon in My Computer.

NOTE I mentioned this in Friday Night's session, but here it is again: the first time you use it, you don't see the full Control Panel; you see a list of a few of the more popular items. You can click the View All Control Panel Options hyperlink to see the whole thing. When you close the Control Panel, it remembers your settings, so the next time you open it, the full Control Panel should appear.

In the rest of the book, I assume you are working with the full Control Panel each time you open it.

2. Double-click the Add/Remove Programs icon.

3. Click the Windows Setup tab. A list of categories appears, as shown in Figure 2.1.

   On the category list, each category has one of the following three check box states next to it:

   ✿ A cleared check box means none of the components in that category are installed.

   ✿ A marked check box with a gray background means that some, but not all, of the category's components are installed.

   ✿ A marked check box with a white background means that all the category's components are installed.

NOTE Two of the categories are not actually categories at all: Address Book and Outlook Express. They are individual components that just happen to be on the Categories list. When you select one of these, the Details button is unavailable because there are no choices to make.

All programs are installed

Some programs are installed

No programs in this category are installed

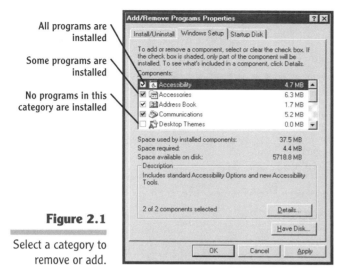

Figure 2.1

Select a category to remove or add.

4. To see the programs in a category, click it and then click Details. A list of programs appears, as in Figure 2.2.

5. Click to turn on/off the check marks next to the programs you want to add or remove.

Figure 2.2

The programs in a category (Accessories, in this example)

If you want to add or remove an entire category as a whole, you can mark or unmark the check box next to the category itself (on the main listing shown in Figure 2.1).

   6. Click OK to return to the category list.

   7. Go through all the categories, selecting and deselecting as desired.

   8. Click OK to accept your choices.

   9. If prompted, insert the Windows Me CD-ROM and click OK. (You might not see that prompt, depending on what you are adding/removing).

Depending on which components you are changing, you might be prompted to restart Windows. Choose Yes if prompted; Windows might not work correctly if you don't.

So why did I teach you this? Because not all the programs I'm going to be talking about in the rest of this session may be installed on your PC. If you run across one that you don't have, you can use the preceding procedure to install it.

Creating and Saving Text Files

Notepad and WordPad are the two text editors that come with Windows Me. A text-editing program lets you type, edit, and save text in a file. Both of these programs are on the Start, Programs, Accessories menu.

Notepad is a plain-text editor, which creates and saves text in a format called ASCII—in other words, plain text with no bold, no italic, no special fonts, and so on. ASCII text is used for computer batch files, for system configuration files, and to distribute text to people who use different computer systems that don't recognize formatting. You will probably not use Notepad much—I just wanted to tell you that it was there.

WordPad, in contrast, is a simple word-processing program that lets you apply formatting to your text. You can use WordPad as a substitute for a full-featured word processor like Microsoft Word. It's free, after all, and other word processors cost extra.

WordPad provides a great introduction to Windows programs, so let's take a few minutes to explore it. Even if you think you won't ever use WordPad, don't skip this part, because I'll be using WordPad to teach you some file-handling essentials.

Typing and Formatting Text

If you have never used a word processor before, follow these steps. They walk you through creating and formatting a document in WordPad.

1. Choose Start, Programs, Accessories, WordPad. The WordPad program opens.

2. Type the following text:

    I love working with my computer! I can spend all day typing and editing text. There's nothing I would rather be doing right now.

    Notice that the text wraps to the next line automatically when you reach the edge of the box. That's called word wrap. You don't need to press Enter except to start a new paragraph.

3. Select the word "love." To select, click and drag the mouse pointer across the text. It becomes highlighted (white letters on black background).

4. Click the *I* button on the toolbar, making the selected text italicized. Then click away from the word to deselect it.

5. Click the Align Right button. The entire paragraph now aligns with the right margin. See Figure 2.3.

6. Select the whole paragraph. (Shortcut: triple-click the paragraph.) Then open the Font drop-down list and choose Times New Roman (Arabic).

7. Open the Font Size drop-down list and choose 14. The text changes to 14-point in size. Click away from the text to deselect it. Figure 2.4 shows the result.

Figure 2.3

The WordPad document after some basic formatting

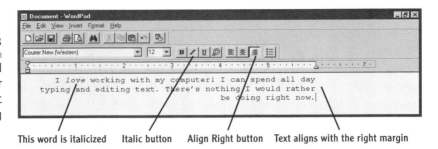

This word is italicized   Italic button   Align Right button   Text aligns with the right margin

Figure 2.4

The text is now Times New Roman font and 14-point in size.

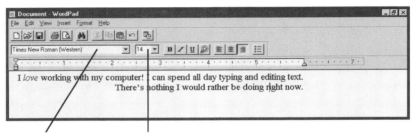

Font drop-down list   Font Size drop-down list

Now you know, in a nutshell, how a word processor works. They all work approximately the same way. There are toolbars with buttons that apply various formatting attributes, and most of the buttons have equivalent menu commands. You can usually find out what a button does by pointing at it to see its name pop up in a ScreenTip.

Saving Files

Saving your work is important so that you can reopen the file again when you need it. All programs save and open files in approximately the same way, so learning about it in WordPad will give you a jumpstart on whatever other programs you'll use.

The first time you save a file, you're prompted for a name and location for it. When you resave the same file later, it uses the same settings without prompting you.

Practice saving a file in WordPad by doing the following:

1. Choose File, Save or click the Save button on the toolbar. The Save As dialog box opens. See Figure 2.5.

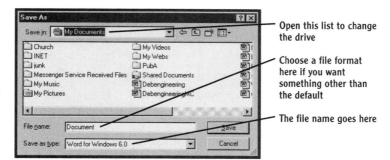

Open this list to change the drive

Choose a file format here if you want something other than the default

The file name goes here

Figure 2.5

Use the Save As dialog box to specify a location and name for the file.

2. The default save location appears in the Save in box. If you want to choose a different location, do the following:

   A. Open the Save in drop-down list and choose the drive on which you want to save. A list of all the folders on that drive appears.

   B. Double-click the folder in which you want to save.

   C. If that folder contains subfolders, they appear; double-click to move to a subfolder if desired.

   There are a couple of buttons in the Save As dialog box that can help you along when displaying the save location you want:

   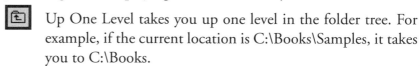 Up One Level takes you up one level in the folder tree. For example, if the current location is C:\Books\Samples, it takes you to C:\Books.

   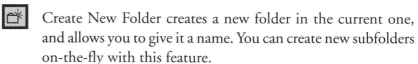 Create New Folder creates a new folder in the current one, and allows you to give it a name. You can create new subfolders on-the-fly with this feature.

   When the Save in location is correct, next turn your attention to the file name.

3. Type the name for the file in the File name text box.

4. (Optional) If you want to save the file in a different format, open the Save as type drop-down list and choose a different type.

Usually you will save the file in the native format of the program in which you create it. For example, WordPad's default format is Word for Windows 6.0. However, you might sometimes want to choose a different type in order to share a file with someone who does not have the same program as you. This is more of an issue with other word processing programs than with WordPad.

5. Click the Save button to save the file.

Starting a New File

In most programs, you start a new file automatically when you start the program. But you can also start a new file at any other time too.

In WordPad, as in most programs, there's a New command on the File menu, and also a New button on the toolbar. You can use either one.

In WordPad, when you start a new document a box appears giving you a choice of file formats. The default is usually the best choice. Not all programs do this, however.

Some programs, such as Microsoft Word, give you a list of templates to choose from if you use the File, New command, but simply start a new, blank document if you click the New button on the toolbar.

Try it out now in WordPad:

1. Click the New button.

2. If you are prompted to save your changes in the file you were working with, choose No.

3. When the New dialog box prompts you for a file format, click OK.

● ●

NOTE WordPad can have only one file open at once; when you start a new file or open an existing one, the previously open file closes. Some other programs allow multiple documents to be open at once. In such programs there is usually a Window menu to allow switching between them.

● ●

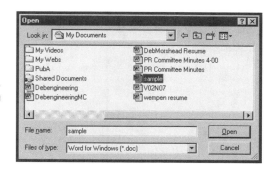

Figure 2.6

The Open dialog box has a lot in common with the Save As box.

Opening Files

Opening files is almost exactly like saving them, except instead of assigning a file a name, format, and location, you are retrieving a file with a certain name and format in a certain location.

For example, to open the file in WordPad that you just saved a few pages back, do the following:

1. Choose File, Open or click the Open button on the toolbar. The Open dialog box appears. See Figure 2.6.

2. If the folder in which you saved the file does not appear in the Look in box, navigate to the correct drive and folder, just as you did when saving.

   Remember, to do so, choose the drive from the Look in drop-down list and then double-click to move through the folders to the desired location.

3. Click the file name on the list of files in that location and then click Open, or simply double-click on the file name.

Printing Your Work

One last thing: printing. Most programs allow you to print your work, and WordPad is no exception.

There are two ways to print: You can choose File, Print or you can click the Print button.

Printer

Number of copies

Print range

Figure 2.7

Make your printing selections here and then click OK.

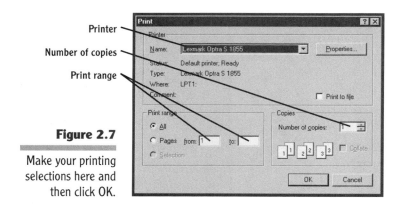

The Print button prints one copy of the entire document on the default printer, without asking you for any settings. The File, Print command, on the other hand, opens a Print dialog box, from which you can choose a page range, a number of copies, a printer (if you have more than one), and so on. See Figure 2.7.

Now you're primed and ready to work with files in almost any Windows-based program! You know how to enter and edit text, and you can save and open files. These essential skills will take you far; you'll be glad you spent the time to master them upfront.

But text files aren't particularly interesting, are they? So let's move on to a topic that's a lot more fun: graphics.

Getting and Editing Graphics

I love to play around with graphics on my PC. I like downloading pictures from the Internet, taking pictures with my digital camera, scanning photos to put on my Web pages, and all the rest of that stuff. If you do too, you'll appreciate Windows Millennium's graphics acquisition and editing tools.

Working with Scanners and Digital Cameras

In earlier versions of Windows, to run a scanner or to copy pictures from a digital camera, you needed to use the software that came with the device. Windows Millennium has changed that, however, by providing direct access to many of the most popular scanner and camera models.

If you upgrade to Windows Me from Windows 95 or 98, and you already had a scanner or camera installed with its own software, that software will still be there, and you can continue to use it normally. But if you install a new scanner or camera after installing Windows Me, the new Windows-integrated interface for the device will be the default.

For some devices, you must go ahead and install the driver software that comes with the device in order for it to work to its best capability. For example, I bought an Intel PC Camera Pro Pack, and when I hooked up the camera to my USB port, Windows Me recognized it immediately and it worked. But the image quality was bad. So I installed the software that came with it, and the image quality got much better.

Another example: When I installed my Umax Astra 2100U scanner, Windows recognized it right away, and it worked perfectly. The scanner came with a CD, so I went ahead and ran its setup program. The setup program included a driver for the scanner and several photo-editing programs. I installed it all. The driver didn't seem to work, but because Windows was capable of running the scanner by itself, that didn't matter. So I uninstalled the driver and kept all the photo-editing programs.

Testing and Configuring Your Scanner or Camera

Is your scanner or camera already installed in Windows? To find out, do the following:

1. Choose Start, Settings, Control Panel.

2. Double-click Scanners and Cameras. A list of currently installed scanners and cameras appears.

3. If yours appears on the list, double-click it to view its properties.

If it's not on the list, see Appendix A for help installing its driver. (Or you can try installing it yourself now by double-clicking Add Device and following the prompts.)

4. Click the General tab if it is not already on top. See Figure 2.8.

5. Click the Test button.

   The exact name of the button varies. Depending on the device, it might be labeled *Test Scanner or Camera*, or just *Test Camera*, or just *Test Scanner*. The test takes only a moment, and a box appears telling you whether it passed.

6. Click OK in the results box. If the device passed, you're all set. If not, see Appendix A for troubleshooting help.

7. Click the other tabs to see what other settings are available. The settings (and tabs) depend on the device model and type.

   For example, some scanners that have quick scanning buttons allow you to customize the buttons on the Events tab, so you can define what program receives the scan when you press each button. Other scanners and cameras don't allow any such customization here.

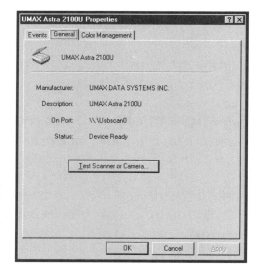

Figure 2.8

Open the Properties for the scanner or camera and display the General tab.

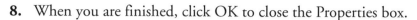

8. When you are finished, click OK to close the Properties box.

You're ready to use your scanner or camera! See the following sections for details.

Scanning a Picture

The directions I'm about to give you apply only if your scanner is directly supported by Windows Me. For all other scanners, you must use the scanning software that comes with the device, and the steps will be a little different.

● ●

NOTE Some scanners might appear to work with Windows Me (that is, they might show up in the Scanners and Cameras window in the preceding section's test) but they won't work when you actually try to scan something with the following procedure. If that's the case, fall back to using the scanner's own software.

● ●

To scan a picture, follow these steps:

1. Place the picture on the scanner bed and close the lid.

2. Choose Start, Programs, Accessories, Scanner and Camera Wizard.

3. If you have more than one scanner or camera, a box appears asking which you want to use. Click the scanner you want and then click OK. The Scanner and Camera Wizard runs.

● ●

NOTE Wizard: A step-by-step series of dialog boxes that helps you accomplish a complex task.

● ●

4. Click Next to begin.

5. The Region Selection box appears, and the scanner scans a preview of your picture. It appears in the Preview area, as shown in Figure 2.9.

6. If needed, adjust the original on the scanner bed and click the Preview button again to preview it.

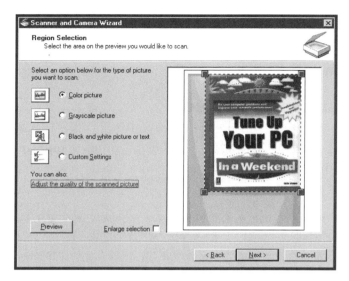

Figure 2.9

The scanner automatically previews your scan.

7. Choose an option button for the image type you want: Color picture, Grayscale picture, Black and white picture or text, or Custom Settings.

8. (Optional) To crop the preview so that only a portion of the image gets scanned, drag the red squares in the corners until only the portion you want to keep is enclosed.

9. (Optional) To fine-tune the scan, click the Adjust the quality of the scanned picture hyperlink. Then make fine-tuning selections in the Advanced properties dialog box, and click OK to return.

   Some of the fine-tuning you can do includes changing the scan resolution (higher is better, but results in a larger image file) and adjusting the brightness and contrast.

10. Click Next to move on. The Picture Destination box appears (Figure 2.10).

11. Enter a name for the picture in the Save picture using this name box.

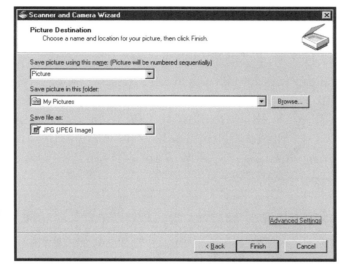

Figure 2.10

Choose where to store the scanned image.

The name you enter can be the same for every picture you scan; Windows will tack a number on to the end of the name so that each picture has a unique name. For example, if you leave the default name here of "Picture," the first picture will be Picture001, the second one Picture002, and so on.

12. Choose a destination folder for the picture, or leave the default My Pictures selected.

The My Pictures folder is inside your My Documents folder, accessible from the Desktop.

13. Choose a file format for the picture, or leave the default format as JPEG.

Different programs accept different picture file formats. JPEG is a good choice because many programs accept it, including most Web sites.

14. Click Finish. The scanner scans the picture (for real this time, not just a preview, so it might take a little longer), and Windows saves it to a file as you indicated.

What can you do with a scanned picture? Lots of things. You can import it into any program that accepts pictures, such as Microsoft Word, FrontPage, or Excel, to dress up your work in that program. You can also e-mail the file to a friend to share the picture, or print it (making your scanner work like a copier!), or fax it (if you have a fax modem and faxing software for Windows).

Transferring Images from a Digital Camera

There are several kinds of digital cameras out there on the market, and Windows interacts with each kind a little differently.

- Some digital cameras are little video cameras that remain attached to your PC full-time. You can use them for video teleconferencing, or to record live video feed from nearby your computer (limited only by the length of the cord).

- Some digital cameras are like regular go-anywhere cameras, except they don't use film but instead record the images digitally. You hook up the camera to the PC to transfer the images to your hard disk.

- Some digital cameras record the images they take on floppy disks, so you never have to hook them up to your PC; you simply take the floppy out of the camera and put it in your PC's floppy disk, and then copy the files from disk to disk.

Windows does not directly support the last type, but it doesn't have to—the camera is never hooked up to the PC anyway. Of the other two types, Windows supports only certain models. (Again, visit http://www.Microsoft.com/hcl to find out if yours is supported.)

If your camera is directly supported, you can use the following procedure to transfer images from it. If not, you must use the software that came with the camera to do that.

1. Hook up the camera to the PC if it's not already connected.

   Some cameras connect via a Universal Serial Bus (USB) interface; others connect through some other port or through a special interface card that they come with. I assume for now that you have already installed the needed connection.

2. If the camera requires you to do anything special to it to place it in transfer mode, do so. For example, some camera models require you to flip a switch or turn a dial.

3. Choose Start, Programs, Accessories, Scanner and Camera Wizard.

4. If you have more than one scanner or camera, a box appears asking which you want to use. Click the scanner you want and then click OK. The Scanner and Camera Wizard runs.

5. Click Next to begin. The pictures currently stored on the camera appear in thumbnail (miniature) view. See Figure 2.11.

6. Delete any of the pictures that you want to remove from the camera without saving. To delete one, click it and press Delete on the keyboard.

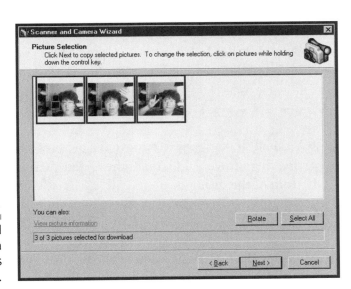

Figure 2.11

The pictures stored on the camera appear as thumbnails.

7. To rotate a picture, click it and click the Rotate button.

8. Select the pictures that you want to transfer to your hard disk. Selected pictures appear with a dark blue border around them; click the Select All button to choose them all, or hold down the Ctrl key as you click each one you want.

9. Click Next to move to the Picture Destination box. It's almost the same as the one shown in Figure 2.9.

10. Enter a name for the pictures in the Save picture using this name box.

   As with the scanner, the name you enter will be the same for every picture, with a number on the end. Windows will tack a number on to the end of the name so that each picture has a unique name. For example, if you leave the default name here of "Picture," the first picture will be Picture 001, the second one Picture 002, and so on.

11. Choose a destination folder for the picture, or leave the default My Pictures selected.

   The My Pictures folder is inside your My Documents folder, accessible from the Desktop.

NOTE Click the Advanced Options button in step 11 to open a box in which you can choose to create a subfolder within My Pictures, with either the name that you entered in step 10 or today's date for the name of the folder.

12. (Optional) If you want to remove the pictures from the camera after saving them to your PC, mark the Delete pictures check box at the bottom of the dialog box.

13. Click Finish.

The pictures are saved to your hard disk, and the folder in which you saved them appears with thumbnail views of the pictures. You can use the buttons above the preview pane to work with the picture. See Figure 2.12.

Rotate the picture

Print the picture

View the picture
preview in its own
window

Zoom in or out

Preview of selected
picture

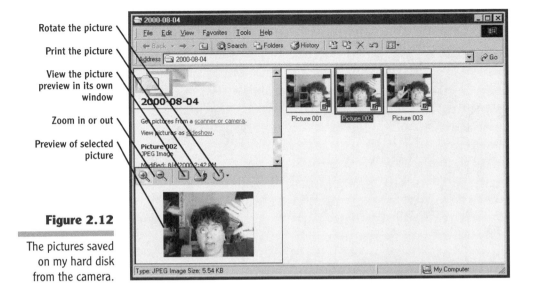

Figure 2.12

The pictures saved
on my hard disk
from the camera.

If you have a video-type camera that doesn't store pictures, you can still use it with Windows, but you'll do so through the Explore Camera feature instead.

1. If you have started the Scanner and Camera Wizard but were told that the picture has no images stored in it, click the Explore Camera hyperlink.

   Or, to explore the camera without going through the Wizard, double-click its icon in My Computer.

   A window appears with a preview of the camera's video feed in one corner.

2. If you want to take a still photo with the camera, click the Take Picture hyperlink. The picture appears below the preview pane. See Figure 2.13.

Now you can use the full Scanner and Camera Wizard to save the still pictures you've taken with your video camera. It'll work the same as if you had a real digital camera.

Click here to take a
still photo

Still photos you've
taken appear
down here

Click here to work with
a picture you've taken

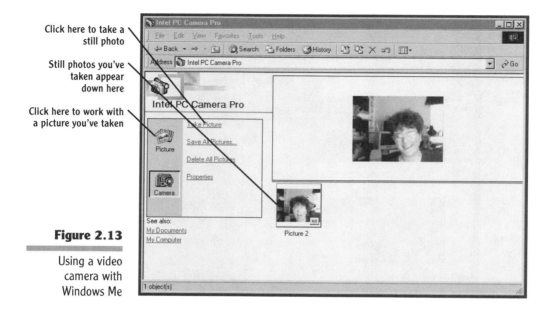

Figure 2.13

Using a video
camera with
Windows Me

If you don't want to bother with the Wizard to transfer the video camera's still pictures to your hard disk, you can do the following instead:

1. In the Explore Camera window, click the Picture icon, changing the list of hyperlinks to those that manage pictures rather than the camera itself.

2. Click the Save All Pictures hyperlink. The picture is saved there with a default name (Picture 1, Picture 2, Picture 3, and so on).

Using the Imaging Program

Windows comes with a program called Imaging that allows you to edit your pictures. With Imaging, you can rotate them, print them, and even add captions and annotations. You can also scan directly into Imaging, or acquire images from your digital camera directly into it. Figure 2.14 shows Imaging with a scanned picture loaded. To start Imaging, choose Start, Programs, Accessories, Imaging.

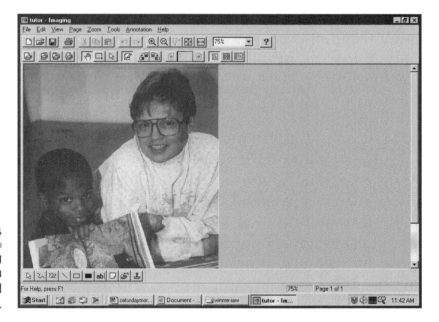

Figure 2.14

The Imaging program helps you acquire and annotate images.

 NOTE Imaging is not a general-purpose photo-editing program. You won't find features here like color adjustment, cropping, or drawing/painting. For such features, use Paint (covered later in this chapter) or a third-party program such as Paint Shop Pro (available for free trial from http://www.jasc.com).

Imaging will open graphics in lots of different graphics formats, but some of its features are not available unless you're working with a TIF or AWD format image. In addition, you can save your work only in TIF, AWD, or BMP format. TIF and BMP are standard graphics formats, and AWD is a fax graphic format.

To scan directly from Imaging:

1. Choose File, Select Scanner.

2. Choose the scanner or camera you want to acquire from, and click OK.

3. Choose File, Scan New or click the Scan New button on the toolbar. The Scan dialog box appears. You've seen these controls before; they're just like in the Wizard.

4. Place the picture to be scanned on the scanner bed, and then click the Preview button to do a test scan.

5. Drag the red squares to adjust the scan area, and set any other scanning options desired; then click Scan to scan the picture and send it to Imaging.

Once the picture is in imaging, you can use the buttons on the toolbar to modify it.

I won't get into every single button and feature here, because you can easily try them out on your own, but here are a few highlights:

Select: Lets you define an area of the image by dragging a rectangle around it.

Drag: Lets you move a selected part of the image by dragging it.

Rotate Left: Rotates the entire image (or the selected portion) to the left 90 degrees.

Rotate Right: Rotates the entire image (or the selected portion) to the right 90 degrees.

But wait—I've saved the best for last. The Imaging program really shines in its ability to *annotate*—that is, to superimpose over the top of an image. You can add explanatory text to a picture, for example, such as writing the names of the various relatives in an old photo underneath each person.

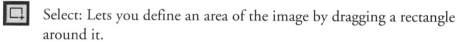

 NOTE   If the commands on the Annotation menu are unavailable, it's probably because the image isn't in the right format. Save your work in TIF format, and they'll appear.

Annotation is so important that it has its own menu and toolbar. (The toolbar buttons correspond one-to-one with the menu commands, so you can use either one.)

If the Annotation toolbar doesn't appear at the bottom of the program window, click the Annotation Toolbar button to turn it on, or choose View, Toolbars and select it from the Toolbar dialog box.

Here are the annotations you can do:

![Freehand line icon]	Freehand line
![Highlighter icon]	Highlighter
![Straight line icon]	Straight line
![Hollow rectangle icon]	Hollow rectangle
![Filled rectangle icon]	Filled rectangle
![Text icon]	Text
![Attach-a-note icon]	Attach-a-note
![Text from file icon]	Text from file
![Rubber stamp icon]	Rubber stamp

To apply one of the annotation effects, click the button you want (or choose one from the Annotation menu) and then click the image or drag across it. The exact procedure depends on the animation chosen. For example, if you choose the Text annotation, you click the image and then type the text. Figure 2.15 shows some of the annotations in place.

Using the Paint Program

Paint is a simple, general-purpose graphic creation and editing program that includes several features that Imaging does not. If you need to touch up a graphic, or replace one color with another, or erase parts of an image, Paint is the right tool for the job.

 NOTE If you want a more powerful all-purpose graphics program, try Paint Shop Pro or Photoshop. If you want a program that's specifically designed for working with scanned photos, try PhotoDeluxe.

Attach-a-note
(solid background)

Typed text
(clear background)

Figure 2.15

Some annotations
done in Imaging

To start Paint, choose Start, Programs, Accessories, Paint. You can open an existing graphics file to edit, or you can create a new picture.

When you create a new picture, the screen is your blank canvas. You choose a color, a tool, and any special attributes for the tool (such as the thickness of your "brush"), and then you drag on the canvas to create your art. As you can imagine, kids love playing with Paint this way! Figure 2.16 shows Paint with a simple picture created.

To use the basic drawing tools in Paint, you click on a drawing tool, and then click on the color that you want to use with it. To choose a background color, right-click; to choose a foreground color, left-click. Then with each of the tools on the drawing area, drag with the left mouse button to use the foreground color, or drag with the right mouse button to use the background color.

Here are the Paint tools. If you make a mistake while drawing or editing, you can press Ctrl+Z to undo your last tool usage.

Figure 2.16

Anyone can draw
simple pictures with
Paint.

 **Free-form Select.** Selects an irregularly shaped area. Used to mark an area for removal or copying. After selecting an area, you can press the Delete key to get rid of it or choose Edit, Copy to copy it, and then Edit, Paste to paste it.

Select. Same as Free-form Select, except it selects a rectangular area.

Eraser. Erases whatever you drag across, replacing it with the currently selected background color (that is, whatever color you right-click on in the color palette). If you use the right mouse button when dragging, you replace the selected foreground color with the selected background color, ignoring all other colors.

Fill. Fills whatever enclosed area you click on with the foreground color (left-click) or background color (right-click). Make sure the area you click on is fully enclosed, or the fill will "leak" into the background.

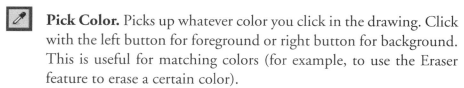

Pick Color. Picks up whatever color you click in the drawing. Click with the left button for foreground or right button for background. This is useful for matching colors (for example, to use the Eraser feature to erase a certain color).

Magnifier. Zooms in and out. Left-click to zoom in; right-click to zoom out.

Pencil. Draws a free-form line with the foreground color. Makes a plain, precise line.

Brush. Draws a free-form line, but you can choose from a variety of brush shapes that make different strokes.

Airbrush. Spray-paints like an aerosol can of paint. Hold down the mouse button to spray.

Text. Places text in the drawing. Click where you want to type the text, and then type.

Line. Draws a straight line.

Curve. Draws a curve. Draw a straight line with this tool and then drag the middle of the line to make the curve.

Rectangle. Choose between border only (no fill), fill only (no border), or both. Hold down Shift to draw a perfect square.

Polygon. Draws a free-form shape of multiple straight lines. Double-click to connect the beginning of the shape to the end to complete the shape.

Ellipse. Same controls as the Rectangle tool but you're drawing an oval or circle. Hold down Shift for a perfect circle.

Rounded Rectangle. Like a Rectangle but the corners are rounded.

Just for practice, try drawing a shape in Paint by following these steps:

1. Choose File, New to start a new drawing.

2. Click the Rectangle tool, and then click the second rectangle option (the filled rectangle with a border around it).

Hold down Shift while drawing to ensure a perfect square

Choose a filled rectangle with a border

Set the background to yellow and foreground to dark blue

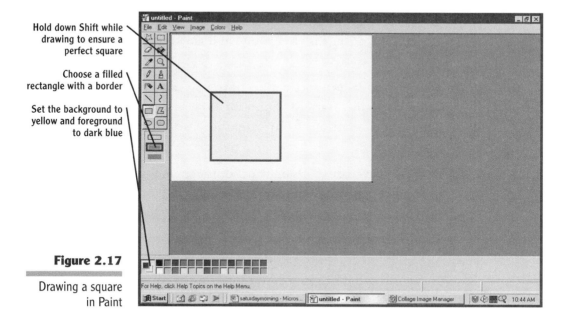

Figure 2.17

Drawing a square in Paint

3. In the color palette, right-click on pale yellow and left-click on dark blue.

4. Move the mouse pointer to the drawing area, and holding down the shift key, drag to draw a square. See Figure 2.17.

Now experiment on your own with the Paint tools. Here's an idea: see if you can turn your basic square into a picture of a house, complete with a slanted roof, windows and doors, and a big round sun in the sky.

Playing Media Clips with Windows Media Player

Earlier versions of Windows had a program called Media Player, but it was simple and plain. The Media Player in Windows Millennium Edition, however, is a real powerhouse.

The new Media Player includes these capabilities:

⚙ You can play media clips including videos, music, sound effects, and others, in any of dozens of different formats.

⚙ If you have an Internet connection, you can explore an online Media Guide section with free sound and video clips to download from your favorite artists.

⚙ If you have an Internet connection, you can listen to hundreds of Internet Radio stations. Some of these are online broadcasts of your favorite stations from around the world; others are Internet-only stations.

⚙ You can play audio CDs on your computer and use play features like track selection, random play, and so on.

⚙ You can copy tracks from your audio CDs to your hard disk so you can listen to them while you work without having the CD inserted.

⚙ You can organize your sound clips from various sources into custom playlists, creating your own "mixes."

You can start Media Player by doing any of the following:

⚙ Click the Media Player icon in the Quick Launch toolbar (to the right of the Start button).

⚙ Double-click the Media Player icon on the desktop.

⚙ Choose Start, Programs, Accessories, Entertainment , Windows Media Player.

When you start Media Player, the Media Guide page appears by default, and pulls the latest content from the Internet to display on that page. The buttons at the left correspond to each of the pages available; you can click a button to go to that page. See Figure 2.18.

Media Player is such a feature-rich program that I could spend the whole morning talking about it! But I'll limit the discussion here to a few of the most useful and fun features, and let you discover the rest on your own later.

Using the Media Guide

Start with the Media Guide because you're already there; that's where Media Player opens up (Figure 2.18). You can skip this part if you aren't connected to the Internet.

Click on any of this content to check it out, just as with a Web page

Click one of these buttons to do something else

Figure 2.18

Windows Media Player, with the Media Guide page displayed.

You can click any of the links on the Media Guide page to listen to or watch clips from the featured artists. You can also browse a huge library of clips from your favorite artists by entering the artist name in the LOOKITUP box.

Notice also that there are four tabs across the top of the Media Guide page: Home, Music, Radio, and Broadband. Click on a tab to check out the additional pages.

NOTE Broadband: A fast connection to the Internet, such as cable or DSL. If you have a standard modem connection to the Internet, you will probably not want to explore the content on the Broadband tab because it will take too long to download.

Listening to Internet Radio

Imagine if you could listen to almost any radio station, anywhere in the world, with no static and no antenna problems. That's what Internet Radio is about. You'll be amazed at the quality and variety of programming available.

Internet Radio in Media Player

There are two ways to listen to Internet Radio in Windows Me. One is to use the Radio toolbar in Internet Explorer; the other is to use Media Player. Because you're already in Media Player, take a look at that method first.

1. Click the Radio Tuner button in Media Player to bring up a searchable list of radio stations.

2. In the Station Finder panel (the right panel), open the Find By list and choose how you want the stations displayed.

   For example, to find only jazz and blues stations, choose Format from the Find By list, and then choose Jazz and Blues from the Select Format list.

3. When you find a station you want to try, double-click on it. See Figure 2.19.

Information about the chosen station

First choose what criterion to filter by

Next choose the filter for that criterion

Sort by any of these columns by clicking them

This indicator shows the station is still loading

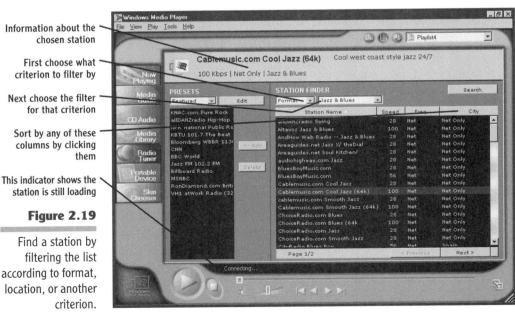

Figure 2.19

Find a station by filtering the list according to format, location, or another criterion.

You can also find by language, location, call letters, frequency, or any of several other criteria.

If you have a slow Internet connection, it might take several minutes before the station begins to play. You also might experience some pauses or choppiness in the play on a slow connection. Broadband Internet users should not experience these problems.

Why does a station take so long to load? It's because Internet Radio is a streaming audio format. The music is transmitted to your PC just in time for it to be played in Media Player. On a slow PC, the least little delay can result in a choppy playback, so Media Player creates a *buffer*, a storage area for several seconds of incoming data. That way if there is a delay in transmission, the music continues to play out of the buffer while your PC catches up, and there is no interruption in the broadcast. The slower your Internet connection, the longer it takes to fill the buffer initially.

NOTE When you double-click a station to play it, a Web page might appear in a separate Window with advertising for that station. You can close this window; the station will continue to play.

To choose a different station, simply double-click a different one, choosing a different filter for the list as needed.

Just like on a car radio, you can create presets for your favorite stations. Media Player comes with a list of presets called Featured, which you see in the left-hand pane in Figure 2.19. You can't edit this list, but you can create your own list of favorite stations by doing the following:

1. Open the Presets drop-down list and choose My Presets.

2. Find a station that you like in the right pane (see the preceding set of steps).

3. Click the Add button to move that station into the My Presets list. See Figure 2.20.

Choose My Presets from
this drop-down list

It has been added to
the My Presets list

This station is selected

Stop button stops the
broadcast

Figure 2.20

Save shortcuts to
your favorite
stations in the
Presets list.

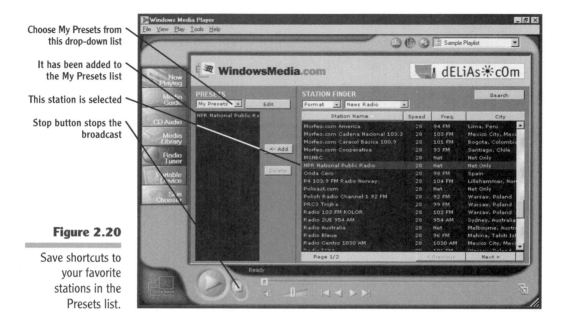

From then on, you can simply double-click the station from your My Presets list whenever you want to listen to it. To stop the station from playing entirely (for example, if the phone rings and you need silence while you take the call), click the Stop button at the bottom of the screen, shown in Figure 2.20.

To create other preset lists, do the following:

1. Click the Edit button in the Presets pane. The Edit Preset Lists dialog box opens.

2. To create a new list, enter a new name in the Add new list box and then click the Add button. For example, Figure 2.21 shows a new list called Talk Radio added.

3. To create a Presets list consisting of the radio stations in your area, enter your ZIP code in the Create local station list box and then click Add. Then click OK at the confirmation box that appears.

4. To move the new list up or down in the list of lists, click on it and then click the Up or Down arrow buttons.

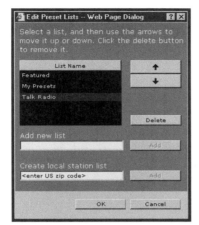

Figure 2.21

Create new preset lists that you can populate with your favorite stations.

NOTE The Featured list can't be moved or deleted, and you can't move any other lists ahead of it. That means, unfortunately, that it's the default list that appears each time you open Media Player. It contains stations that have paid a fee to Microsoft to be featured.

5. When you are finished editing, click OK.

Internet Radio in Internet Explorer

The other way to use Internet Radio is to turn on the Radio toolbar in Internet Explorer and use its controls to find a station. This method uses fewer system resources, so it can come in handy if you want to do something else while the radio is playing (like play a processor-intensive game). Follow these steps to play a radio station through Internet Explorer:

1. Start your Internet Connection, and start Internet Explorer. (Double-click the Internet Explorer icon on your desktop; see the Sunday Morning session if you need to set up Internet access.)

2. Choose View, Toolbars, Radio. The Radio toolbar appears.

3. Click the Radio Stations button on the toolbar, and choose Radio Station Guide from the drop-down list that appears.

Stop button
Radio toolbar
Volume control

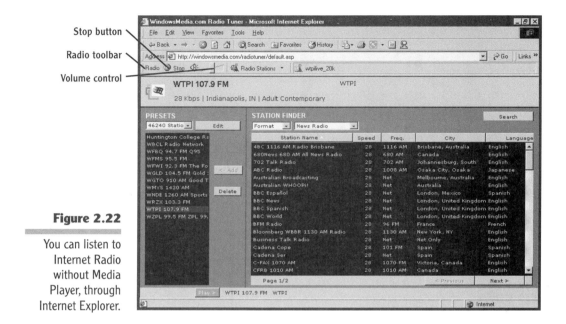

Figure 2.22

You can listen to Internet Radio without Media Player, through Internet Explorer.

A Radio Station Guide Web page opens in Internet Explorer, as shown in Figure 2.22. Notice how much it looks just like the station guide you saw in Figure 2.20.

4. Select the station you want to play, and double-click it to start it playing.

5. Use the Presets list to add the station to your list of favorites, just as in Media Player.

Here's another way to store radio station favorites in Internet Explorer. Click the Radio Stations button on the Radio toolbar and choose Add Station to Favorites. Then enter a name for the station in the box that appears and click OK. The station will then appear on your Favorites list in Internet Explorer. In addition, if you reopen the Radio Stations list from the Radio toolbar, you'll see that the station now appears on that menu as well.

Playing Audio CDs

When you insert an audio CD in your CD-ROM drive, Media Player launches itself and begins playing the CD. (If it doesn't start automatically, you need to turn on AutoInsert Notification, as described at the end of the Saturday Afternoon session.)

● ●

NOTE Some audio CDs have custom computer programs on them, and inserting the CD in a computer plays that program. If that's the case with a CD, Media Player won't start automatically. Exit from the CD's own program, and then manually start Media Player.

● ●

As the CD plays, you can change to any other tab in the Media Player. It will continue to play.

The most common tabs you will want to use during CD play are Now Playing and CD Audio. You can use the Now Playing tab when playing any format (Internet radio, CDs, digital audio clips, and so on), but I think it's the most fun with CDs.

Working with the Now Playing Controls

The Now Playing tab lists the CD tracks to the right, with a visualization in the center, and the player controls at the bottom. See Figure 2.23.

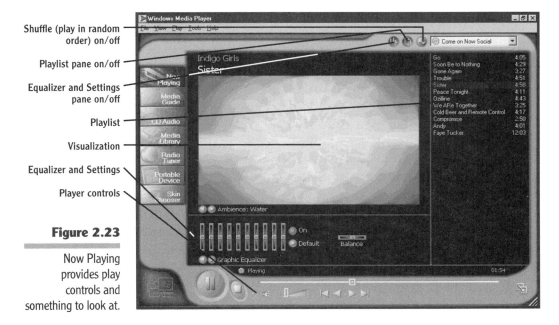

Shuffle (play in random order) on/off

Playlist pane on/off

Equalizer and Settings pane on/off

Playlist

Visualization

Equalizer and Settings

Player controls

Figure 2.23

Now Playing provides play controls and something to look at.

• •

Visualizations: A very cool feature of the new Media Player; they are patterns, colors, or other moving images that react to the music. You can click the right and left arrow buttons under the current visualization to change it, or choose Tools, Download Visualizations to get more from the Microsoft Web site.

• •

The Player controls, shown in Figure 2.24, work just like on a regular CD player or cassette tape deck. You can pause, stop, fast-forward, rewind, and so on. The Volume and Seek controls are sliders you can drag to the left or right; all the others are buttons to click. There are also equivalent menu commands on the Play menu for each of the player controls.

From the Now Playing tab, you can also:

✿ Change to different controls in the Equalizer and Settings area by clicking the right and left arrow buttons under it, or turn off that pane entirely by clicking its on/off button (see Figure 2.23).

✿ Double-click a track on the playlist to jump to that track.

✿ Change the visualization by clicking the right and left arrow buttons under it, or choose View, Visualizations and then choose one from the submenus.

✿ Click the Shuffle button (see Figure 2.23) to play the tracks in random order.

✿ Resize any of the panes by dragging the divider line between two panes.

Figure 2.24

Player controls work just as you expect them to on any audio-playing device.

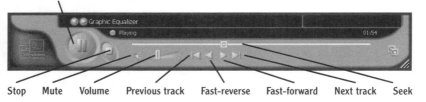

Pause (changes to Play when paused)

Stop   Mute   Volume   Previous track   Fast-reverse   Fast-forward   Next track   Seek

Turn on/off any of the panes with the buttons in the top-right area of the player, or with the commands on the View, Now Playing Tools submenu.

Working with the CD Audio Controls

Now move on to the CD Audio tab. From here, you can select individual tracks to play or not, and copy tracks to your hard disk for later listening when you no longer have the disc in your drive. (This takes up a lot of hard disk space, however—at least a few megabytes per song.) Figure 2.25 provides a first look at the CD Audio tab.

NOTE If you like listening to the CD from the Now Playing tab but you want to select only certain tracks to play, go to the CD Audio tab and select the tracks, and then go back to Now Playing. The CD will continue to play.

Figure 2.25

The CD Audio tab offers some additional controls and activities for working with a CD.

A check mark appears beside each song on the CD Audio tab, along with details about the track such as time, genre, and artist. If there's a certain track you don't want to hear, deselect its check box and it won't play.

Here are some other ways to edit the playlist:

⚙ Right-click a track and choose Edit and then edit its name. This changes the name as it appears in the playlist but does not affect the CD itself in any way; CDs are read-only.

⚙ Change the order in which tracks will play by right-clicking a track and choosing Move Up or Move Down.

Copying CD Tracks to Your Hard Disk

Here's the feature that many of you are probably waiting eagerly to learn about: the ability to copy a CD to your hard disk for later listening. Media Player copies each track in WMA (Windows Media Audio) format, rather than the more popular MP3 format. That shouldn't be a problem as long as you use Media Player to listen to the tracks, rather than some other player.

NOTE You can buy Walkman-like devices that play digital audio clips, but the most popular format accepted by these devices is MP3. Some portable media players support WMA format too, however, and others allow you to record by hooking them into your sound card or USB port, so the original format of the clip is not an issue. See the documentation for your device to find the best way of transferring CD audio tracks to your portable digital music player.

To copy tracks to your hard disk:

1. On the CD Audio tab, select all the tracks you want to copy. Remove the check mark next to any you don't want.

2. Click the Copy Music button. The Copy Status column shows the copy progress, as in Figure 2.26, and the button changes to Stop Copy.

When the tracks have been copied, they show up on the Media Library tab, discussed in the next section. And when you view them on the CD

Copy Music/Stop Copy
button

This track is being
copied

This track is waiting to
be copied

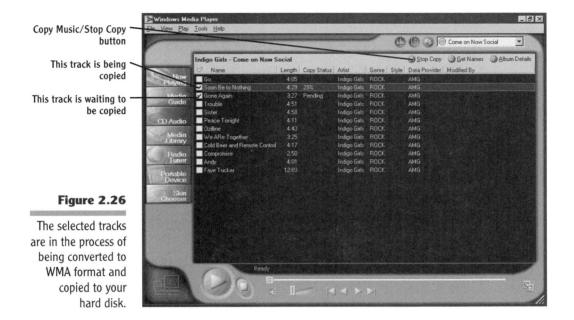

Figure 2.26

The selected tracks
are in the process of
being converted to
WMA format and
copied to your
hard disk.

Audio tab, the Copy Status column shows Copied to Library. By the way, it's perfectly okay to copy your own CDs for your own use; it becomes illegal when you distribute them to other people.

NOTE If you want to copy tracks to your hard disk in MP3 format rather than WMA, there are a variety of free and shareware utilities available that do so. Check out http:// www.shareware.com to find one. Media Player will play MP3 files, so once the files are on your hard disk, you can use them in Media Player the same as WMA files.

Organizing Clips in the Media Library

Head on over to the Media Library tab, where you can manage all your various types of music in one place. I've saved this tab for last because it can be the most complex, especially if you have music from lots of sources.

The Media Library tab has a folder tree, just like in Windows Explorer. I've expanded all the branches of the tree in Figure 2.27 so you can see what's

Figure 2.27

The Media Library helps you organize your music clips.

there. So far, the only clips I have are the two tracks I copied from the CD in the preceding section. You can see them categorized in various ways on the folder tree: by Artist, by Genre, and by Album. All Audio, which is selected in Figure 2.27, shows a master list of all clips in your library.

To play a clip, simply double-click on it, the same as usual. To remove a clip from the Media Library, right-click on it and choose Delete from Library.

Adding Tracks to Your Media Library

As you saw in the preceding section, copying tracks to your hard disk from CDs is one way to get songs into your Media Library. Another way is this:

1. Choose File, Add to Library, Add File. An Open dialog box appears.

2. Locate and select the file you want to add from your hard disk. Refer back to "Creating and Saving Text Files" earlier in this chapter if you need some help working with files.

3. Click Open. The song is added to your library.

Figure 2.28

This song I've added to my library is a little short on details about itself.

Depending on how the file was created, it might not have all the information that a CD-copied track contains. For example, the track in Figure 2.28 has the artist name and the song name both together in the Artist column, and there's no information about genre.

Editing a Clip's Information

You can edit a clip's information to provide the details if you know them. To do so:

1. Right-click the clip and choose Edit. The Name field becomes editable.

2. Type over the current name, or click to move the insertion point into it and edit it.

3. Press Tab to move to the next column (Artist), and type the artist name.

4. Press Tab and continue to the next column, completing all the columns as desired.

5. Click away from the clip to take it out of editing mode.

Automatically Adding Many Tracks at Once

You're probably thinking that adding all your clips to the Media Library is going to be a big chore, right? Wrong. Media Player has a feature that searches your hard disk and adds all the clips it finds automatically.

◆ ◆

Some games come with sound clips for various sound effects in the game, and these will be added to the Media Library too if you go the automatic route described next. You can avoid this by limiting the search to certain folders on your hard disk (the ones where you know your music clips are), or by excluding certain file formats from the search, such as WAV, which is the format that many game sound effect files are in. And you can always remove a clip from the library later if you don't want it there.

◆ ◆

To search your hard disk for clips to add:

1. Choose Tools, Search Computer for Media. The Search Computer for Media dialog box opens.

2. Open the Search for media in drop-down list and choose the drive on which you want to search (when you have more than one hard drive and your clips are all on one of them).

3. If you don't want to search the entire drive, click the Browse button next to Beginning in, select the folder in which you want to start, and then click OK.

   This will search the chosen folder and any subfolders within it, ignoring the rest of the drive.

4. (Optional) To omit Windows-supplied WAV and MIDI files from the search, leave the Include WAV and MIDI files found in system folders check box unmarked.

5. When you have selected the search options you want (see Figure 2.29), click Start Search. The search begins.

6. When a message appears that the search is complete, click Close. Then click Close again to close the Search box. The new clips now appear in your Media Library.

Figure 2.29

Search your hard disk for clips to automatically add to the Media Library.

Organizing Clips into Playlists

The full list of your clips can become a little bit unwieldy as you add more and more clips from your CDs and from other sources. That's where custom playlists come in handy. You can create a playlist that contains your favorite tracks for various occasions, like "Mellow Music" or "Party Mix," and then load and play that playlist quickly whenever you want it.

To create a playlist:

1. Click the New Playlist button in the toolbar.

2. Enter the name for the new playlist and click OK.

    Now the new playlist appears in the folder tree. Scroll down near the bottom of the folder tree, and find My Playlists. Click the plus sign to expand it if needed, and you'll find your new, empty playlist there.

3. Browse the Media Library and select a file that you want to copy to your playlist.

4. Scroll the folder tree pane so that your playlist is visible, and then drag the track from the Media Library and drop it onto the playlist.

5. Repeat steps 3 and 4 to add other tracks to your playlist.

Here's another way to add a track to a playlist: select the track and then click the Add to Playlist button on the toolbar. A menu opens containing all your playlists; click the one you want to add it to. Pretty easy, eh?

TIP To add the currently playing track to the displayed playlist, click the Add button above the listing (looks like a plus sign) and on the menu that appears, choose Add Currently Playing Track.

Now that you have a playlist, here's what you can do with it:

- To move a track around in the playlist, simply drag it up or down on the list. Or right-click it and choose Move Up or Move Down. There are also Move Up and Move Down arrow buttons above the track listing.

- To remove a track from the playlist, select it and press the Delete key, or right-click it and choose Delete from Playlist. There's also a Delete button above the track listing; clicking it opens a menu of deletion options.

Changing the Appearance of Windows Media Player

So far in this chapter, you've seen the default Media Player in all the figures. But you can radically change its appearance through the use of a feature called *skins*. When you apply a skin to the player, it works the same as always but the controls look different. Figure 2.30 shows an example of a different skin.

Click here to return to full window view

Click here to shrink to mini-view

Point to a button to see a ScreenTip telling what it does

You can also click here to return to full window view

Figure 2.30

A skin makes the Windows Media Player look different, but it still works the same.

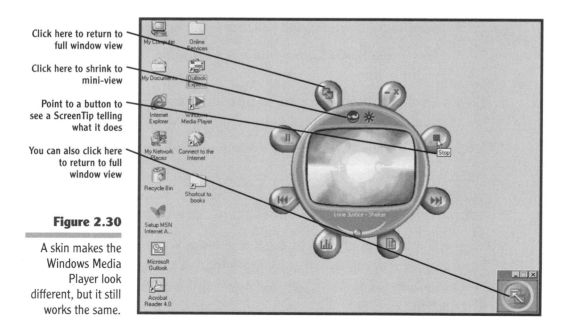

Figure 2.31

The Media Player with a skin applied, shrunk to a smaller size on the desktop.

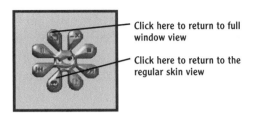

To select a different skin, display the Skin Chooser tab. Pick a skin, and then click Apply Skin. You can get more skins from the Microsoft Web site by clicking the More Skins button.

Some skins allow you to shrink them so they take up less space on your desktop. For example, the skin shown in Figure 2.30 can be reduced to the one shown in Figure 2.31 by clicking the button above the visualization window that looks like a face.

Take a Break

Windows Media Player is so much fun, you might find yourself playing with it all morning! But let's move ahead, because there's a lot to cover before lunchtime. So set some tunes to play while you take a snack break, and then come back here to learn about Windows Movie Maker when you're ready.

Using Windows Movie Maker

Windows Movie Maker is another new feature in Windows Me. It helps you organize multimedia clips—that is, pictures, videos, soundtracks, voice narrations, and so on—into movies that you can play on your computer monitor, store on your hard disk, and e-mail to friends and family.

Suppose, for example, that you have video footage of little Tommy taking his first steps. You can hook up your video camera or VCR to your computer (with the right equipment, of course) and create a digital video clip out of that footage. You can then edit that clip and combine it with a soundtrack and voice-over narration.

In order to use motion video footage, you need a way of getting the footage into your PC. One way is to buy a video interface device (Dazzle is one brand) that plugs into an open slot on your motherboard or connects to your USB port. Its purpose is to translate analog footage, such as from a video camera or VCR, into a digital file on your PC. Another way is to use a digital video camera to record the video. Such cameras typically come with their own interface for importing content into your PC.

A movie need not include video footage, however. If you have a scanner or digital camera, you can import still images from it, and you can also create a movie out of images you've acquired from other sources such as the Internet. A movie with still photos is somewhat like a slide show, with each image remaining on the screen for a few seconds and then being replaced by the next image.

The music for your movie soundtrack can come from a music clip stored on your hard disk. You can copy one from a CD-ROM (as explained earlier in this session), or use a clip (such as an MP3 file) that you have downloaded from a Web site.

If you have a sound card and a microphone to plug into it, you can record voice narration for your movie. This is different from a soundtrack, and plays "on top of" the sound track at the same time.

Here are the steps for creating a movie:

1. Import the content for the show into Windows Movie Maker collections. These collections are not movie-specific; they can be drawn from over and over.

2. Start a new movie, and arrange the video clips or still photos in the order in which you want them.

3. Add a soundtrack if desired.

4. Record voice narration if desired.

5. Preview your movie and then save it to your hard disk.

In the following sections I'll show you how to accomplish each of these steps. But first, you'll need to start Windows Movie Maker. To do so, choose Start, Programs, Accessories, Windows Movie Maker.

> **NOTE**   The first time you start Windows Movie Maker, a tour window appears. You can run through the various parts of the tour if you like, or you can click Exit to skip it and rely on the steps in this book instead.

Creating Collections

You can save all your content in the same collection, or you can create different collections for each type of content or for content on a particular subject. Collections are a lot like folders in Windows Explorer (see the Friday Evening session for a review of that).

To create a new collection:

1. On the folder tree, click the collection into which you want to place the new one. (By default this is the top-level collection, called My Collections.)

2. Choose File, New, Collection or click the New Collection button on the toolbar.

3. Type a name for the new collection and press Enter.

Now, whenever you are recording or importing content in the following sections, simply make sure the desired collection is selected before you record or import.

Recording New Content

You can record new content for your show right from within Windows Movie Maker. The recording process depends on what input devices you have.

Recording Video Clips

With a digital video camera, you can feed directly into Windows Movie Maker from the camera. You can also take still pictures using your digital video camera.

If you have a regular video camera that records onto tape, you'll need some sort of interface device to connect it to your PC. It might work directly with

Windows Movie Maker, or it might require you to use the software that comes with the interface to first save the video to your hard disk. If that's the case, see the upcoming section, "Importing Existing Content from Disk."

NOTE Digital video cameras need not be expensive. I'm using a $100 Intel model that plugs into my USB port, and it works just fine with Windows Movie Maker. Its only drawback is that it must stay attached to the PC in order to function; I can't take it outside to capture footage.

To record from a digital video camera, follow these steps:

1. Ensure that your video camera is connected to your PC, and that your PC recognizes it. (See "Testing and Configuring Your Scanner or Camera" earlier in this chapter.)

2. In Windows Movie Maker, choose File, Record, or click the Record button on the toolbar. The Record dialog box opens. See Figure 2.32.

3. Open the Record drop-down list and choose what you want to record: Video Only or Audio and Video.

Preview pane shows what the camera currently sees

Take Photo button (still photo)

Record button (motion video)

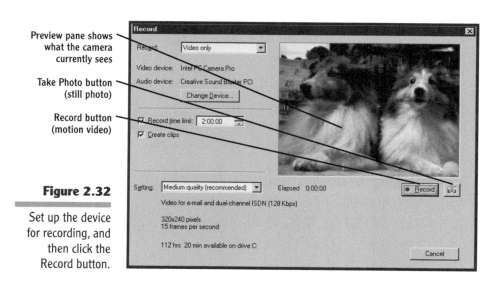

Figure 2.32

Set up the device for recording, and then click the Record button.

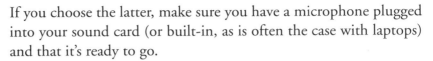

If you choose the latter, make sure you have a microphone plugged into your sound card (or built-in, as is often the case with laptops) and that it's ready to go.

4. If the desired video and audio device names don't appear, click the Change Device button, select the devices to use, and click OK.

NOTE You can also set the camera settings in step 4; click the Change Device button, select the device, and then click the Configure button to open the Properties box for the camera. Different cameras have different settings, but you might find settings there for automatic light adjustment, for example, or for color correction.

5. Change any of the following options as desired:

   ⚙ Set a Record time limit if you want to limit the size of the clip being recorded. (Clips take up a lot of space on your hard disk.)

   ⚙ Choose Create clips if you want the video feed broken into separate clips every time it detects a different frame (such as when you turn the camera on, or turn off the Pause feature). Otherwise the entire video feed will be stored in a single clip.

   ⚙ Choose a quality setting. The default is Medium; higher quality will record more frames per second, but will take up more storage space on your drive and will take longer to transmit when you e-mail the movie to someone later.

6. When you are ready to record video, click the Record button.

   Or, if you want to take a still photo using your video camera, click the Take Photo button instead and then skip to step 8.

7. When you are finished recording, click the Stop button. The Save Windows Media File dialog box appears, in which you can name your clip.

8. Enter the name you want to use for the clip, and click Save.

NOTE ●
Video clips are saved in the WMV format (Windows Motion Video); still clips are saved in the JPG format.
● ●

The clip now appears. Depending on its content, Movie Maker might break it into more than one clip; if so, each clip appears as a separate item in a folder with the clip name you specified when you saved.

For example, in Figure 2.33, the clip has been broken into three parts. "Dogs" was the name I used in saving. (It would not have done this splitting if I had not chosen the Create clips option in step 5.) The fact that the clip is split is not a problem because when you assemble the movie, you can place each clip adjacent to one another so it appears to be one long video piece. Splitting merely adds flexibility to the movie-assembly process.

Video clips

All are stored in a common collection

Figure 2.33

A recorded video called "dogs" has been split into three separate clips.

NOTE You can also manually split a video clip into one or more separate clips. To do so, play the clip by double-clicking it, and at the desired split point, click the Split button (the rightmost button in the toolbar beneath the video preview pane).

Recording Sound Clips

Recording a sound clip is just like recording a video clip, except you use only your microphone. To do this, you must either have a built-in microphone on your PC (which is often the case with laptops) or a microphone attached to the Mic port on your sound card.

Follow these steps to record a sound clip with your microphone:

1. Choose File, Record or click the Record button on the toolbar. The Record dialog box opens.

2. Open the Record drop-down list and choose Audio Only.

3. If your sound card name doesn't appear next to Audio Device, click the Change Device button, select it, and click OK to return.

4. Set the record quality or any other desired options, as described in step 5 of the preceding set of steps.

5. Click the Record button, and begin speaking or making noise into the microphone.

6. Click the Stop button when finished. The Save Windows Media File dialog box opens.

7. Enter the file name to use. The file will be saved in WMA format (Windows Media Audio).

8. Click Save. The clip is created and placed in the collection.

Importing Existing Content from Disk

You can import existing movies, videos, music, sounds, still images, or music files into your collections.

Importing existing content is the same regardless of the content's format. Windows Media Player accepts content in a wide variety of formats, including all popular digital movie formats such as MPEG, WMV, and AVI. It also accepts many sound and graphic file formats too.

To import content:

1. Display the collection into which you want to import.

2. Choose File, Import. The Select the File to Import dialog box appears.

3. Locate and select the file you want to import.

    To narrow down the list of files, you might want to choose a file type from the Files of Type drop-down list. By default, all importable files are shown. See Figure 2.34.

4. Click Open to import the file.

If you find that you have accidentally imported the file into the wrong collection, you can easily drag it to another collection, just as you do when managing files in Windows Explorer.

Figure 2.34

Choose a file to import into a collection.

Starting a New Project

Now that you have imported or recorded the content for your movie, you are ready to start assembling it in a project, which you'll save in Windows Movie Maker.

What's the difference between a project and a movie? Well, when you publish the project as a movie, you create a read-only copy that you can never edit again; that's why it's important to save the project as well as the movie. The project continues to be editable, so you can always make changes and re-publish the movie whenever you like to reflect those changes.

You can assemble a project in any order, but I like to start with the visual images (video clips and still photos), and then add the soundtrack. Then finally, as the last step, I add the voice narration.

A new, empty project starts when you start the program, but you can start a new project at any time by doing the following:

1. Choose File, New Project or click the New Project button on the toolbar.

2. If prompted to save your changes to the existing project, click Yes or No and save (or not), as appropriate.

Adding Clips to the Project

Start your project by dragging clips from your various collections into the timeline at the bottom of the screen.

There are two views of the project: Storyboard and Timeline. You can add audio clips only to Timeline view. If you attempt to drop an audio clip on the Storyboard, a message will appear telling you that it is switching to Timeline view automatically; click OK to go on. To switch manually between Storyboard and Timeline views, you can use the View menu or click the buttons to the left of the project area.

Figure 2.35 shows a project in-progress in Storyboard view. Notice that only the pictures and video clips appear. The same project viewed in Timeline view, in Figure 2.36, shows that there is an audio soundtrack included too.

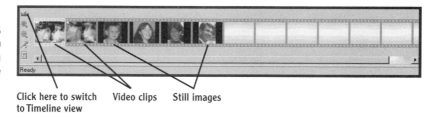

Figure 2.35

A project in
Storyboard view

Click here to switch   Video clips   Still images
to Timeline view

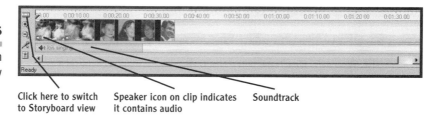

Figure 2.36

The same project in
Timeline view

Click here to switch   Speaker icon on clip indicates   Soundtrack
to Storyboard view   it contains audio

To remove a clip from the project, click it on the timeline or storyboard
and press the Delete key. To move it around on the project, drag it to the
left or right.

Setting Trim Points for a Video Clip

If you want to use only a portion of a video clip, you have a couple of
options. You can split the clip and then use only one of the split portions,
or you can trim the clip. Trimming is active only for the current project,
whereas splitting splits the clip in the collection, so it will continue to be
split if you use it later in another project.

To set the trim points for a clip, do the following:

1. Add the video clip to the project, either on the Storyboard or the
   Timeline.

2. Make sure the clip is selected (again, on the Storyboard or Timeline).

3. Click the Play button beneath the video preview pane, and when
   the clip reaches the part where you want it to begin, choose Clip, Set
   Start Trim Point or press Ctrl+Shift+Left Arrow.

4. Allow the clip to continue playing, and when it reaches the part where you want it to end, choose Clip, Set End Trim Point or press Ctrl+Shift+Right Arrow.

Everything between the two trim points will appear in the movie; everything else will not.

Changing the Duration of a Still Image

When you import a photo, it is assigned a default duration. The original setting is five seconds, but you can change the default duration by choosing View, Options and entering a different value in the Default Imported Photo Duration box. The photo's default duration is always the setting that was in effect when it was imported, however. So, for example, if you import a photo when the Default Imported Photo Duration is set to five seconds, and then you later change that setting to 10 seconds, all photos you imported prior to the change will remain with five-second durations.

You can change a still picture's duration on the timeline, however, for each individual usage of it. Do the following:

1. View the workspace in Timeline view.

2. Click the picture for which you want to change the duration. Trim handles appear above it, as shown in Figure 2.37.

3. Drag the ending trim handle (the one on the right) to the left to make the picture appear for fewer seconds, or to the right to make it appear for more seconds.

Mouse pointer becomes a double arrow

Figure 2.37

Adjust the trim for a picture to control its duration in the movie.

4. If the picture was not on the end of the timeline, and you increased its duration, the picture to its right might now be partially obscured. Select that picture, and then drag its beginning trim handle (the one on its left) so that the two pictures do not overlap anymore.

Creating Transitions

You probably noticed in the preceding section that it's possible to overlap two objects on the timeline. When you overlap objects, you create a transition effect between them, so that one fades into the other. It's a pretty neat effect, and certainly looks better than simply replacing one image with the next.

● ●

Windows Movie Maker does not allow you to choose between different transition effects. If that is an important feature to you, and you are working with still images only, try a program like PowerPoint for assembling your presentation.

● ●

To create a transition effect, simply make the clips overlap slightly. You already saw how to adjust the clip's trim in previous sections.

You might find it helpful when trying to precisely adjust trimming to zoom in. Use the plus and minus buttons to the left of the workspace to zoom in or out on the project. For example, Figure 2.38 shows the project zoomed in. Notice how much easier it is to see the overlap amounts when zoomed in.

Zoom in   Zoom out

Figure 2.38

Zoom in to work precisely with the timeline.

Adding a Soundtrack

To add a soundtrack, drag a sound clip onto the workspace. If you are not already in Timeline view, it switches for you automatically, and a box informs you that it's happening.

You can trim the soundtrack the same as any other object. Select it, and then drag its trim handles, or trim it by playing it and setting start and end trim points as you learned to do for videos earlier in the chapter.

Setting Audio Levels

If the video track has its own audio in addition to the audio tracks you are adding, the two can easily conflict with one another unattractively. You can fix this problem by adjusting it so that one or the other is dominant. To do so:

1. Click the Adjust Audio Level button or choose Edit, Audio Levels.

2. Drag the slider to control the relative volume levels between the two tracks. See Figure 2.39.

3. Click the Close (X) button on the dialog box to close it.

Recording Narration

After you've finalized the durations of each clip, you're ready to record your narration. You won't want to record it earlier, because if the durations of the clips change, the narration will be off.

Figure 2.39

Choose the relationship of audio levels between audio and video soundtracks.

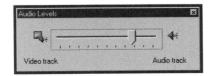

To record narration:

1. Prepare your microphone and ensure that it's working.

 2. Click the Record Narration button to the left of the timeline, or choose File, Record Narration. The Record Narration Track dialog box appears.

3. Set any of the following options:

   ⚙ If the device and line are not correct as shown, click the Change button and select the correct ones. The Device should be your sound card, and the Line should be the line into which your microphone is plugged (probably Mic Volume).

   ⚙ If you want to mute the video soundtrack while the narration is speaking, mark the Mute Video Soundtrack check box. Otherwise the two will play on top of one another.

   ⚙ Adjust the recording level using the Recording Level slider if desired. Use the meter next to the slider as a guide.

4. When you are ready, click Record. Your presentation begins showing itself in the preview pane.

5. Speak into the microphone, narrating as you go along.

6. When you are finished, click Stop. The Save Narration Track File dialog box appears.

7. Enter a name for the narration track, and click Save. (The track is saved in WAV format.)

If you had a soundtrack, you might find that the narration has forced the soundtrack to move over on the timeline. To have them play simultaneously, drag them so that they overlap.

Previewing the Movie

Before you publish the movie, you will want to preview it to make sure everything is as you want it to be. To preview the movie in the Preview pane, simply click the Play button while the first frame of the project is selected in the workspace. To view it full-screen, click the Full Screen button beneath the preview pane or choose Play, Full Screen.

Saving Your Movie

Ready to publish the movie? First, save your project. Remember, you can't make changes to a published movie, so if you want to change it, you'll need to make changes to the project and then republish. To save your project, choose File, Save or click the Save button on the toolbar, and save as you do any other data file in a program.

Now you're ready to make a movie! To do so:

1. Choose File, Save Movie. The Save Movie dialog box opens.

2. Choose a quality from the Setting drop-down list. The default is Medium.

NOTE If you will be distributing the movie via the Internet, keep the quality at medium or lower to keep the file size small. If you will be distributing it on a CD or playing the movie on your own PC, and you have plenty of disk space, use a higher quality. You can check the file size in the File size area of the dialog box. See Figure 2.40.

3. Enter any information desired in the Display information area. All this information is optional. See Figure 2.40.

4. Click OK. The Save As dialog box appears.

5. Enter a file name for your movie in the File Name box.

6. Click OK. Your movie is saved, and a message appears asking whether you want to watch it now.

7. Click Yes to watch the movie or No to return to Windows Movie Maker.

And that's all there is to making your own movies! Pretty simple, eh? Windows Movie Maker is not a terribly sophisticated program, and there are a

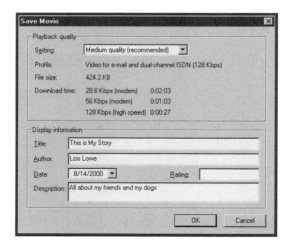

Figure 2.40

Enter information about the movie.

lot of "better" video-editing programs on the market today that do more sophisticated things, particularly with transitions. However, because Windows Movie Maker is free, and it does everything that the average home user needs, there's no reason for most folks to look any further.

And the Rest: Other Useful Accessories

Whew! Are you tired of accessories yet? Stick with me if you can; I want to review a few of the minor accessories, so you can see what's available with Windows Me. This won't take long or be painful, I promise.

Calculator

Calculator has been around almost as long as Windows itself! A version of this simple program came with the original Windows back in the early 80s.

Calculator is just what you expect it to be: a full-featured electronic version of the pocket calculator you probably use regularly in school and business. To run Calculator, choose Start, Programs, Accessories, Calculator.

The calculator has two modes: Standard and Scientific. Scientific has many more functions and special features. Figure 2.41 shows the two modes side-by-side so you can compare them. Switch between them by choosing the mode you want from the View menu.

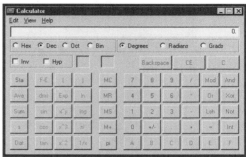

Figure 2.41

Calculator in Standard (left) and Scientific (right) modes

You can use the calculator with the numeric keypad on your keyboard (when NumLock is turned on), with the number keys across the top, or by clicking the number buttons onscreen.

HyperTerminal

HyperTerminal is a communications program that manages direct dial-up connections. This used to be the primary type of program used for going online, back in the days when people used BBSs (*bulletin board services*) instead of Internet service providers. Nowadays, however, there are few reasons to use a program like HyperTerminal. Nearly all companies that used to maintain BBSs for customers now use Web sites for that purpose, and nearly all companies that used to allow dial-up access to their servers by remote employees now employ VPNs (*virtual private networks*) instead.

Nevertheless, I want to make you aware that HyperTerminal is there, in case you should ever run into a situation where someone tells you to use your modem to dial up to a certain system.

To run HyperTerminal, choose Start, Programs, Accessories, Communications, HyperTerminal. If the program isn't there, it probably hasn't been installed yet; see the instructions for adding Windows programs at the beginning of this chapter.

When HyperTerminal starts, it invites you to create a new connection, as shown in Figure 2.42. Just fill in the blanks and follow the prompts to do so. It will then automatically connect using your modem.

Figure 2.42

HyperTerminal
walks you through
creating a new
connection.

When you are finished with the connection, HyperTerminal offers to save your connection. If you choose do to so, the next time you start HyperTerminal, instead of creating a new connection again, you can click Cancel and then use the File, Open command to reopen the saved connection.

Phone Dialer

The phone dialer is useful primarily if your modem and your telephone share the same line. It uses your modem to dial the phone from a directory that you create in the Phone Dialer program.

Many people consider Phone Dialer to be more trouble than it's worth, but you might want to experiment with it. Choose Start, Programs, Accessories, Communications, Phone Dialer to start it up.

To dial a number, enter the number using the onscreen keypad, lift the receiver on your telephone, and click the Dial button.

Phone Dialer has a set of speed dial buttons on the right. To set one up, click on a blank button. A dialog box appears prompting you to enter the number for that button. After working through that setup, you can then dial that number by clicking the button. Figure 2.43 shows Phone Dialer with a couple of speed dial buttons configured.

NOTE   To change a speed dial button that has already been set up, choose Edit, Speed Dial.

Figure 2.43

Phone Dialer uses
your modem to dial
your telephone.

Accessibility Tools

If you have a disability that limits your sight, vision, or mobility, you might find the Accessibility tools and options in Windows helpful.

The Accessibility tools are found on the Start, Programs, Accessories, Accessibility menu. If you don't see them there, use Add/Remove Programs to add them as you learned at the beginning of the chapter.

 NOTE There are two parts to the Accessibility features that you can add and remove in Add/Remove Programs: Accessibility tools and Accessibility options. The tools are the utilities on the Start menu; the options are the features you set through the Control Panel.

The best way to configure the Accessibility tools is with the Accessibility Wizard. Choose Start, Programs, Accessories, Accessibility, Accessibility Wizard, and work through it step-by-step to configure Windows to help you compensate for your unique disability situation. For example, Figure 2.44 shows a screen from this Wizard.

The Accessibility options, which you set through the Accessibility icon in the Control Panel, let you configure the keyboard to make it easier for a person with limited mobility or only one available typing hand to use special functions such as holding down the Shift key. There are also settings for Sound, Display, and Mouse that set up special features to compensate for various disabilities.

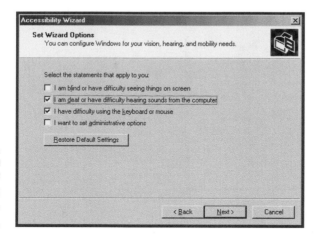

Figure 2.44

The Accessibility
Wizard asks you
questions to help
configure Windows.

Character Map

There are more than 250 characters available in a typical typeface, but your keyboard doesn't have keys for all of them. So what do you do when you want to insert a special character such as a cent sign (¢) or a copyright symbol (©)? Well, some programs have an Insert Symbol feature that you can use, but in programs that don't have that feature, you can rely on the Character Map in Windows. The Character Map copies a symbol from a font onto the Clipboard in Windows, and from there you can paste it into any application.

To access the Character Map, choose Start, Programs, Accessories, System Tools, Character Map. (If it's not there, you'll need to add it with Add/ Remove Programs.)

Once in the Character Map, do the following to select and insert a symbol into another program:

1. Open the Font drop-down list and choose the font from which you want to select a character.

2. Click the symbol you want from the grid of characters that appears for that font.

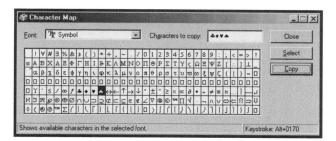

Figure 2.45

Four symbols selected, ready for copying to the Clipboard

3. Click Select to copy that symbol to the Clipboard. You can copy more than one symbol. Figure 2.45 shows four symbols selected, as shown in the Characters to copy box.

4. When you are finished selecting symbols, click the Copy button.

5. Switch to the program into which you want to paste the symbols, and choose Edit, Paste or click the Paste button on the toolbar (if available in that program).

Wrapping Up

Now you're familiar with the Windows accessories, and you know how to use many of the most common ones. You've explored Windows Media Player and Windows Movie Maker, two of the most entertaining additions to Windows Millennium Edition, and you're familiar with working with both text and graphics programs. Congratulations! You've come a long way since you started this morning!

Now that you know how to do all kinds of useful things in Windows, you're ready to play around with Windows' settings. So have some lunch, and in this afternoon's session you'll learn how you can customize Windows using the many settings in the Control Panel.

Customizing Your System

- ✿ Running Programs More Easily
- ✿ Changing the Way Windows Looks
- ✿ Changing the Way Windows Acts
- ✿ Applying Desktop Themes

Windows Me contains an amazing array of customization features that help you set up your screen, your keyboard and mouse, your menus, and just about anything else you can think of, in a way that makes the most sense to you. Because after all, we're all different, right? So it doesn't make sense that everyone would find the same settings useful.

I'll break down this session into three parts, each focusing on a different type of customization:

- ⚙ Launching programs more easily
- ⚙ Changing the way Windows looks
- ⚙ Changing the way Windows acts

Running Programs More Easily

In the next few sections I'll explain ways to set up Windows to let you start programs quickly, without having to wade through multiple levels of menus or search for a program's icon.

Turning Personalized Menus On/Off

Windows Me comes with a feature called Personalized Menus that hides seldom-used commands when you first open the Start menu. Only after you click the down-pointing arrow at the bottom of the menu, or pause for several seconds, does the full menu appear. For example, when I choose Start, Programs on my PC, I initially see the menu shown in Figure 3.1. Then I click the down arrow at the bottom to see the full version, shown in Figure 3.2.

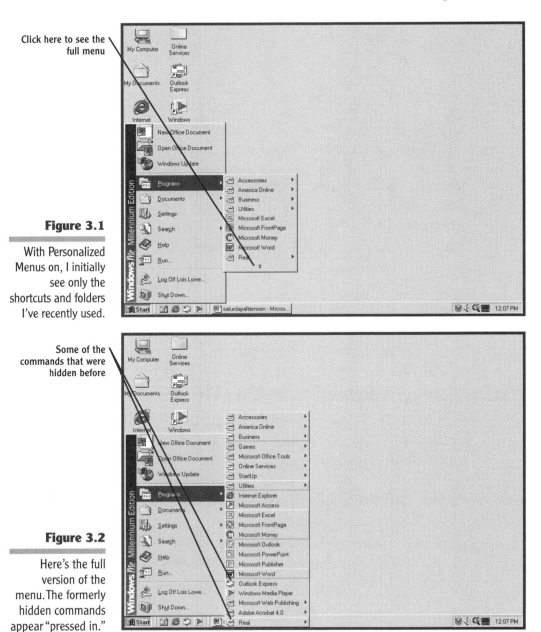

Figure 3.1

With Personalized Menus on, I initially see only the shortcuts and folders I've recently used.

Figure 3.2

Here's the full version of the menu. The formerly hidden commands appear "pressed in."

Each time you choose a command, Windows remembers, and puts that command on the "short list" next time. So eventually, only the programs you use will appear on the initial version of the menu.

If you don't like this feature and want to turn it off—or if it sounds like a great thing but it's currently disabled on your PC—use the following steps to change the setting.

1. Right-click the taskbar and choose Properties.

 NOTE •
Another way to accomplish step 1 is to choose Start, Settings, Taskbar and Start Menu.
• •

2. Select or deselect the Use personalized menus check box. See Figure 3.3.

3. Click OK.

You can also reset the usage data, so that Windows starts again with a default set of commands and folders and starts recording your usage data from scratch. To do so:

1. Right-click the taskbar and choose Properties.

2. Click the Advanced tab. See Figure 3.4.

Turn on/off
personalized
menus here

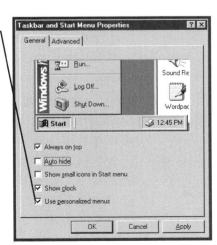

Figure 3.3

Control the way
the Start menu
and taskbar
operate using this
dialog box.

Figure 3.4

The Advanced tab provides a means for clearing the menu usage data.

3. Click the Clear button.

4. Click OK.

NOTE Clicking the Clear button not only clears the menu usage data, but also the Documents menu (Start, Documents).

Organizing the Start Menu More Efficiently

As you install more and more programs, your Start menu can begin to get crowded. The full list in Figure 3.2 was pretty long, for example, and it can get even longer as time goes by. Luckily, you can arrange and organize the programs on the Start menu to make things more compact and tidy.

The Start menu is actually a folder on your hard disk (C:\Windows\Start Menu), and its contents are determined by the folders and shortcuts stored there. For example, the Start menu contains a folder called Programs (C:\Windows\Start Menu\Programs)—that's the Programs menu you see when you click Start and point to Programs. Within that Programs folder is a folder called Accessories, and within Accessories is a folder called System Tools, and so on. When you create, delete, and rearrange submenus, you are actually working with those folders.

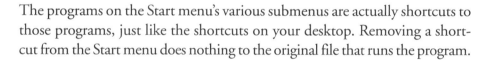
The programs on the Start menu's various submenus are actually shortcuts to those programs, just like the shortcuts on your desktop. Removing a shortcut from the Start menu does nothing to the original file that runs the program.

Rearranging Items on the Start Menu

If you just want to reposition a folder or shortcut on the existing menu system, you can drag it around:

1. Choose Start, Programs. The Programs menu opens.

2. Point to the item you want to move, but don't click it yet.

3. Press and hold down the left mouse button. (Do not release the button yet.)

4. Drag the item to the desired new location on the Start menu or any of its submenus. Point to a submenu to open it. A horizontal line shows where the item is going. See Figure 3.5.

5. Release the mouse button, dropping the item into its new location.

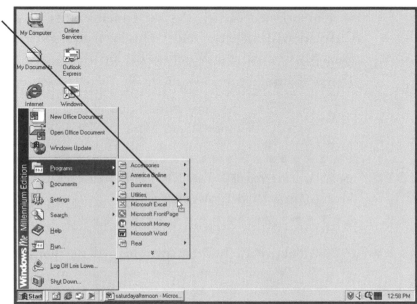

Figure 3.5

Drag an item to reposition it on the Start menu.

Re-sorting the Menus Alphabetically

When you first install a new program, it places itself at the bottom of the Programs menu (or whatever menu it installs its shortcut to). When you restart the computer, it's supposed to alphabetize the menu structure again, but it doesn't always happen. Here's how to re-alphabetize manually:

1. Right-click the taskbar and choose Properties.

2. Click the Advanced tab (Figure 3.4).

3. Click the Re-sort button.

4. Click OK.

Restructuring the Start Menu

You might decide that your entire Start menu organization needs an over-haul. (I do this every six months or so, just for good housekeeping.) For example, perhaps you have a lot of programs installed (as in Figure 3.2), and you need a way of organizing them. Or perhaps you want to consolidate some of the folders, placing the shortcuts for similar programs together in a single folder.

As I mentioned earlier, the Start menu takes its content from the C:\Windows\Start Menu folder. This is a regular folder you can work with using My Computer or Windows Explorer.

To modify the Start menu structurally, follow these steps:

1. Right-click the Start button and choose Explore. This opens the folder C:\Windows\Start Menu in Windows Explorer.

 NOTE Another way to accomplish step 1 is to right-click the taskbar, choose Properties, click the Advanced tab, and click the Advanced button.

2. Double-click the Programs folder. All the shortcuts and folders from the Programs menu appear. See Figure 3.6.

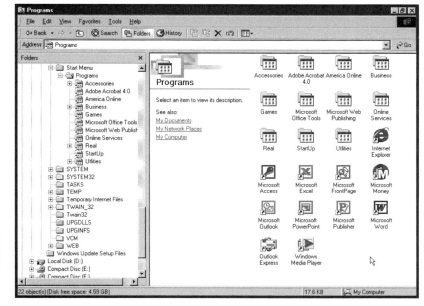

Figure 3.6

Browse the
Programs menu in
Windows Explorer.

3. Change the structure of the Programs menu system by doing any of
    the following:

    ○ Create new folders (File, New, Folder). These become new
      submenus on the Programs menu.

    ○ Drag folders into the new folders you create, or into any other
      folders, to make them into submenus.

    ○ Delete any unwanted folders or shortcuts by selecting them
      and pressing the Delete key.

◆ ◆

CAUTION Do not delete the StartUp folder. This is a special folder used by Windows; any programs
with shortcuts in this folder will load automatically when Windows starts. You can make a
program start automatically by copying its shortcut and placing it here, or prevent a
program from starting at startup by deleting its shortcut from here.

◆ ◆

4. Check your work by opening the Start menu and pointing at various folders to see their content. Close the Start menu by clicking away from it without selecting a command.

5. When you finish editing, close the Windows Explorer window.

If you have accidentally deleted something you decide you want to keep, remember that it's probably still available in the Recycle Bin.

Adding and Removing Items from the Start Menu

In the preceding section you saw how to work with the Start menu contents as folders and shortcuts, and you can create and delete shortcuts from there just as you do with any other files.

However, for those who are a bit intimidated by that level of editing, Windows also offers a wizard for adding shortcuts to the Start menu. Here's how to use it.

1. Right-click the taskbar and choose Properties.

2. Click the Advanced tab.

MENU REORGANIZATION TIPS

Not sure how to reorganize things? Here are some of my favorite strategies.

Create a few new folders with generic names, such as Games, Utilities, and Business. Then drag the shortcuts for various programs into the appropriate folders and delete all those specific folders for each application.

Sometimes you might not want to delete the specific folder for an application. For example, if the folder contains the program shortcut and shortcuts to several related utilities, you might want to keep the folder to keep those shortcuts grouped together. If you want to tidy things up without getting rid of the specific folder, drag the whole folder into one of your generic-named new folders. It then becomes a submenu of it.

If you have a lot of programs that installed directly on the Programs menu, you can create a folder for them and place their shortcuts there instead. For example, Microsoft Office places shortcuts for all its applications on the Programs menu. You can create a folder called Office and move all those shortcuts into it.

3. Click the Add button. A Create Shortcut dialog box opens.

4. Click the Browse button. A Browse dialog box opens.

5. Locate and select the file that runs the program you want to create the shortcut for. Program files usually end in .exe or .com. Then click Open.

6. Back in the Create Shortcut dialog box, click Next to continue.

7. In the Select Program Folder box, select the folder on the Start menu in which you want to place the shortcut. See Figure 3.7. Then click Next.

 NOTE At step 7 you can use the New Folder button to create a new subfolder if desired.

8. Type a name for the shortcut. This is the text that will appear on the menu. Then click Finish.

9. Click OK to close the Taskbar and Start Menu Properties dialog box.

To remove an item from the Start menu, you can delete it from Windows Explorer (as in the preceding section), or you can do the following:

1. Right-click the taskbar and choose Properties.

2. Click the Advanced tab.

Figure 3.7

Choose where the new shortcut is placed.

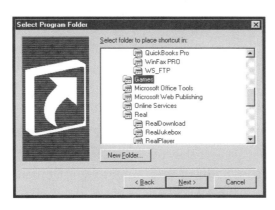

Figure 3.8

Select a folder or
shortcut to remove.

3. Click the Remove button. The Remove Shortcuts/Folders dialog box opens. See Figure 3.8.

4. Select the shortcut or folder to remove, and then click Remove.

5. Repeat step 4 for additional folders or shortcuts; then click Close.

6. Click OK to close the Taskbar and Start Menu Properties dialog box.

In reality, however, you will probably never need to use the preceding steps. Why? Because there's a method that is much easier. To remove an item from the Start menu the easy way, follow these steps:

1. Open the Start menu, and locate the shortcut or folder to remove.

2. Right-click it and choose Delete.

3. Click OK to confirm.

This is the only method I ever use; the others are too slow for my taste.

Other Ways to Customize the Start Menu

Windows Me has a whole slew of options for changing how the Start menu looks and operates. Some of these might seem familiar, but most of these are brand-new to Windows Me.

Figure 3.9

Normal menu icons (left) and small ones (right)

One of the basic settings is the icon size. The default is to show rather large icons next to each menu option on the first level of the Start menu. To change to smaller icons here, right-click the taskbar and choose Properties; then select the Show Small Icons in Start Menu check box. Figure 3.9 shows the large (left) and small (right) icons, so you can see the difference.

The other Start menu options are all accessed from the Advanced tab of the Taskbar and Start Menu Properties box. To set them:

1. Right-click the taskbar and choose Properties.

2. Click the Advanced tab.

3. Select or deselect check boxes as desired in the Start Menu and Taskbar section. Table 3.1 explains each of these settings.

4. Click OK.

Managing Desktop Shortcuts

As you know, your desktop contains shortcut icons to some of the most common programs and file-management windows, such as My Computer, Internet Explorer, and the Recycle Bin. Depending on what programs are installed, you might have other shortcuts there too, such as a game, an online service, or a utility program.

TABLE 3.1 START MENU SETTINGS YOU CAN ADJUST	
Option	**Purpose**
Display Favorites	Includes a Favorites submenu. Useful for quick access to your Favorites menu from Internet Explorer.
Display Logoff	Displays/hides the Logoff command. Turn off to prevent users from logging off during a Windows session.
Display Run	Displays/hides the Run command. Turn off to prevent users from running programs not on the Start menu. (They can still do it from Windows Explorer, but this will slow them down a bit.)
Enable Dragging and Dropping	Allows drag-and-drop editing of the Start menu.
Expand Control Panel	Creates a submenu for the Control Panel instead of opening the Control Panel window.
Expand Dial-Up Networking	Creates a submenu for the Dial-Up Networking folder instead of opening it in a window.
Expand My Documents	Same as above except for the My Documents folder.
Expand Printers	Same as above except for the Printers folder.
Scroll Programs	If there are more programs on a menu than can be displayed in a single column in the current display resolution, a single down-pointing arrow will appear at the bottom of the menu, which can be clicked to scroll down the list. Note that this is different from the double down-pointing arrow in the Personalized Menus feature.

Arranging Icons on the Desktop

You can drag icons around on your desktop, placing them anywhere you like. For example, you might want to move the ones you don't use very often to an out-of-the-way corner. For that matter, you can just delete the ones you don't use often, unless they are system shortcuts that can't be deleted such as My Computer. To delete a shortcut, click it and press the Delete key.

You can also arrange the icons on your desktop according to name, type, size, or date, just like in any other file listing. Right-click the desktop and choose Arrange Icons and then the criterion by which you want to arrange.

If you try to drag an icon around on the desktop but it immediately snaps back into place, the AutoArrange feature is probably turned on. Right-click the desktop and choose Arrange Icons, AutoArrange to turn that feature off or on.

Creating New Desktop Shortcuts

You can create new shortcuts on your desktop too. Desktop shortcuts allow you to bypass the Start menu and start a program more quickly. Most of the time I keep about a dozen shortcuts on my desktop for the programs I use most frequently. Figure 3.10 shows them. Note that most of them have a little arrow in the lower-left corner, indicating that the icon is a shortcut rather than the original file.

◆ ◆

The little arrow in the corner is not a foolproof method of distinguishing a shortcut from the original. Some icons on your desktop, especially those placed there by Windows itself, do not have that little arrow and yet are shortcuts all the same.

◆ ◆

To create a shortcut for a folder or file on the desktop:

1. Locate the file or folder in a file listing (such as My Computer or Windows Explorer).

2. Right-click the file or folder and choose Create Shortcut. A shortcut for that item appears in the same location.

3. Drag that shortcut to the desktop.

Shortcut to a drive

Shortcut to a program

Shortcut to a folder

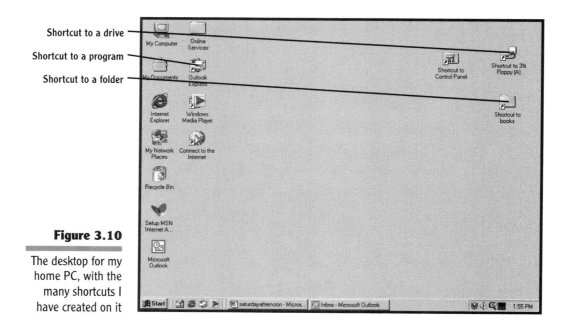

Figure 3.10

The desktop for my home PC, with the many shortcuts I have created on it

To create a shortcut for a drive, do the following:

1. Double-click My Computer on the desktop.

2. Drag the drive icon to the desktop. A message appears stating that you cannot move that drive to the desktop, offering to create a shortcut instead.

3. Click Yes.

Here's an alternative method (possibly quicker): Right-drag the item (file, folder, or drive) onto the desktop from its current location. (Remember, right-dragging is the same as regular dragging except it uses the right mouse button instead of the left.) When you drop it, a menu appears. Choose Create Shortcut(s) Here from the menu. This also works to create shortcuts from programs and folders on the Start menu; simply right-drag them from the Start menu to the desktop.

You can create shortcuts almost anywhere, not just on the desktop. For example, suppose you have a folder called Projects in which you keep the

important files for the project you are working on. One of the projects is a team effort with a friend in another office, so you agree to store all the files for it on your company's network. You can create a shortcut to that folder and store the shortcut in your own Projects folder. That way you can quickly access that network folder when you need it without physically placing a copy of the network folder on your hard disk.

Renaming Shortcuts

Some shortcuts have the words "Shortcut to" in their names, which can be cumbersome. You might want to rename the shortcut to remove that. You might want to rename a shortcut for some other reason too. For example, if you are setting up a shortcut to an installation program for a friend who is not very experienced with computers, a file called Shortcut to Setup32 might be confusing. You can rename that shortcut Double-Click Here to Begin, a much friendlier name for a novice.

Renaming a shortcut is the same as renaming any other file or folder. Select it, press F2, and then type the new name. (Or right-click it and choose Rename from the shortcut menu.)

Customizing the Taskbar

The taskbar, more than any other screen element, helps you run programs and manage the programs and windows that are already open. In the following sections I'll show you some ways to change how it looks and performs to fit your needs.

Customizing the Quick Launch Toolbar

The Quick Launch toolbar is a group of small icons that appears to the right of the Start button. It provides easy access to Internet Explorer, Outlook Express, and Windows Media Player, as well as a shortcut that minimizes all open windows. See Figure 3.11.

The exact buttons that appear on it can differ depending on your setup. Some programs, such as RealMedia Player, add themselves to the Quick Launch toolbar when you install them.

Figure 3.11

The Quick Launch toolbar provides a few quick shortcuts to common programs.

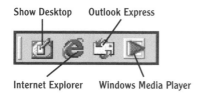

Show Desktop   Outlook Express

Internet Explorer   Windows Media Player

 TIP   The Show Desktop button, shown in Figure 3.11, is handy. It minimizes all open windows so you can see your desktop.

You can add buttons to and remove them from the Quick Launch toolbar as desired. For example, you might add a button that starts your dial-up Internet connection.

If you use a certain few programs a lot, you might want to add shortcuts to them in the Quick Launch toolbar rather than placing shortcuts to them on your desktop. The advantage is that the Quick Launch toolbar is always visible, whereas the desktop might not be. The drawback: the icons on the Quick Launch toolbar are picture only (no words beneath), so if you place two shortcuts there that use the same icon, you might have a hard time telling them apart.

To add a button to the Quick Launch toolbar, do the following:

1. Select the file, folder, drive, or program shortcut you want to place on the Quick Launch toolbar.

2. Drag the item and drop it on the Quick Launch toolbar in the spot where you want it.

To delete a button from the Quick Launch toolbar, right-click it and choose Delete from its shortcut menu.

Displaying Other Toolbars on the Taskbar

Three other toolbars come with Windows; you can display them if you like. However, they take up a lot of space on the taskbar, so you probably do not

want them displayed all the time. Right-click the taskbar, choose Toolbars, and then choose the toolbar you want to toggle on or off. They are as follows:

- ✪ **Address.** Provides an Address box into which you can type URLs and other addresses you want to browse, either on the Web, on your local network, or on your own PC.

- ✪ **Links.** Provides buttons that link to various Web pages.

- ✪ **Desktop.** Provides buttons for the shortcut icons on your desktop, so you don't have to minimize all the windows for access to them.

Experiment with these on your own as desired. (Personally, I don't find them very useful.)

Creating Your Own Toolbars

You can also create more toolbars from existing folders if you want. Right-click a toolbar and choose Toolbars, New Toolbar. Locate and select the folder you want to make into a toolbar and click OK. However, I have never had occasion to need this, and you probably won't either. I simply add all the shortcuts I want to the Quick Launch toolbar.

Changing the Taskbar Size

You can set the taskbar to auto-hide itself, which means it disappears completely except for a thin gray bar until you move your mouse pointer into its area. Then it pops up, ready for use.

To auto-hide the taskbar:

1. Right-click the taskbar and choose Properties.

2. Select the Auto Hide check box.

3. Click OK.

You can also adjust the height of the taskbar. By default it takes up one row, but you can expand it to multiple rows. This can come in handy if you have several toolbars displayed or many windows open at once, because it makes everything less crowded. To change the taskbar height, position the mouse pointer over the top edge of the taskbar and drag upward to increase

Figure 3.12

The taskbar has
been expanded.

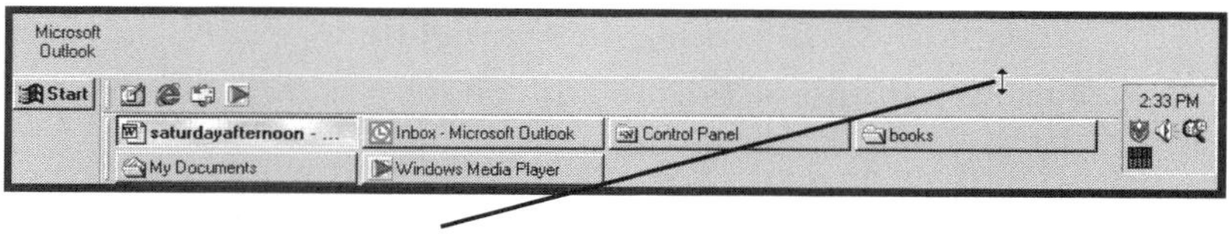

Position the mouse pointer over the top border and drag to change the size.

it or downward to decrease it. Figure 3.12 shows the taskbar expanded to
three rows in height.

Changing the Taskbar Position

The taskbar appears at the bottom of the screen by default, but you can
make it appear at the top or at either side of the display if you prefer.
Simply drag it where you want it.

Take a Break

How does your screen look at this point? Different? Feel free to play with
any of the settings you're learning about in this chapter. You might want to
take some time with them now, before moving on. But wait—there's more.
The video display settings you'll learn about in the following section are a
blast to play with too.

Changing the Way Windows Looks

The display you see onscreen is limited by the capabilities of your video
card and your monitor as a team. In other words, your display looks only as
good as the weaker of those two components can make it look.

The following sections take you through these steps:

 ✪ Making sure Windows correctly identified your video card and monitor

 ✪ Choosing a color depth and display resolution appropriate for your
 needs (and your monitor size)

 ✪ Setting the refresh rate for optimal viewing

Setting Up the Correct Video Drivers

When you install Windows, it's supposed to detect your hardware and install the appropriate drivers. That's called Plug and Play.

Sometimes, however, Windows doesn't perfectly identify a piece of hardware, and so it doesn't load the best driver available. For example, on some PCs, Windows detects the video card as standard VGA, when in fact it is a much better card than that. As a result, you're limited to the standard VGA video resolution and color depth. (More on that later.) For best performance, you should correct Windows' information about your video card, so it can use drivers that enable all the capabilities your video card supports.

Determining What Video Card Windows Thinks You Have

To see what Windows currently thinks you have as a video card, do the following:

1. Right-click the desktop and choose Properties.

2. Click the Settings tab.

3. Look under Display. You should see something like this: {*Monitor name*} on {*Video card name*}. The latter is the video card that Windows thinks you have. For example, in Figure 3.13, it's ViewSonic PT770 on AccelStar II 3D Accelerator.

4. Click OK to close the Properties box.

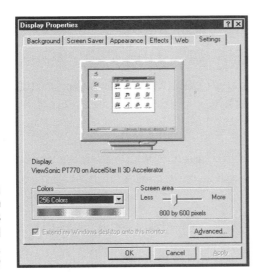

Figure 3.13

Windows reports your monitor and video card. Is it correct?

NOTE To determine whether Windows identified the video card correctly, you must know the right answer yourself. Most people buy the video card as part of a whole PC, rather than buying and installing it themselves. If you aren't sure what kind of video card you have, now is a good time to look through the documentation that came with your PC to find out. Look for a packing slip or receipt that came with the PC that might list it. Or, if you're feeling intrepid, you can also turn off the PC and remove the cover to try to locate a name and model number of the video card itself. Some PCs have video built into the motherboard; if that's the case with yours, look for a chip on the motherboard with the video card name. You can also watch the screen as the PC starts; the first thing it displays is usually the video card make and model.

All this fuss is probably overkill, though. As long as Windows lists a video card name, and not just VGA, it probably has detected your card correctly.

Changing the Video Card Windows Thinks You Have

If the video driver shown in the Display Properties does not match the make and model you think you have, you can try installing a different driver.

If the video card came with a setup program on disk, run that. If it didn't, or if it came with a driver disk with no setup program, follow these steps:

1. Right-click the desktop and choose Properties.

2. Click the Settings tab and then click the Advanced button.

3. Click the Adapter tab and then click the Change button. The Update Device Driver Wizard runs. See Figure 3.14.

4. Choose Specify the location of the driver (Advanced). Then click Next.

   You must do this because Windows doesn't know the correct name of the video card, so it can't search for an updated driver for it automatically.

5. Click Display a list of all drivers in a specific location, so you can select the driver you want. Then click Next.

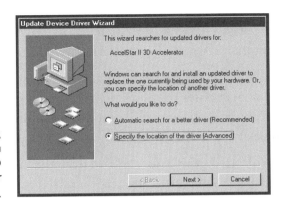

Figure 3.14

Windows offers to find a better driver for your video card.

6. Click Show All Hardware. A list of video card manufacturers and models appears.

7. Choose the manufacturer and model for your card. Or, if it's not listed but you have a disk that came with it, put that disk in your drive and then click Have Disk and locate it.

8. Continue through the Wizard, clicking Next as prompted, until you come to a Finish button; then click Finish to install the driver.

Installing an Updated Video Driver

If Windows identifies your video card correctly but it still isn't working right, perhaps you need to install a newer or better driver for it.

If your video card came with a disk containing a setup program, run that. Always run the setup program with a device if possible, because it might contain some auxiliary programs that can help the device run better, such as DirectX drivers for the specific video card.

If you don't have a setup program for the video card, you can search for a better driver by doing the following:

1. Right-click the desktop and choose Properties.

2. Click the Settings tab and then click the Advanced button.

3. Click the Adapter tab and then click the Change button. The Update Device Driver Wizard runs. See Figure 3.14.

4. Insert the floppy or CD that came with the video card into your PC.

5. Leave Automatic search for a better driver selected and click Next.

6. Windows checks the drivers it finds on disk against the currently installed one, chooses the best one, and presents its findings. Click Finish to accept its recommendation to either install a new driver or keep the existing one.

If you have downloaded a driver for the card from the Internet, perhaps the download contained a setup program. If so, run it. If not, do the following to install the new driver:

1. Right-click the desktop and choose Properties.

2. Click the Settings tab and then click the Advanced button.

3. Click the Adapter tab and then click the Change button. The Update Device Driver Wizard runs. See Figure 3.14.

4. Choose Specify the location of the driver (Advanced) and click Next.

5. Mark the Specify a location check box and enter the path to the downloaded driver in the text box provided. (You can also use Browse to locate it.) See Figure 3.15.

6. Follow the prompts, clicking Next as needed, to follow Windows' recommendation for installing the new driver or keeping the existing one.

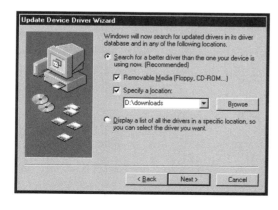

Figure 3.15

Specify where Windows should look for the new driver.

7. When you come to a screen with a Finish button, click Finish to end the driver update.

Configuring Your Monitor

A I mentioned earlier, the overall display quality is limited by the combined capabilities of the monitor and the video card. You just learned how to set up the video card; now it's time to look at the monitor.

Windows probably detected your monitor as a plug-and-play monitor. That's fine, unless your system is capable of higher refresh rates than what is specified by the generic plug-and-play monitor driver. (See "Changing the Display Refresh Rate" later in this chapter for details about that.) For the best quality image onscreen, set up Windows for the specific monitor you have if possible.

Go back to that initial "see what's there procedure" I gave you in the "Determining What Video Card Windows Thinks You Have" section, and see what monitor Windows reports. If it's correct, you're done.

If the monitor name is not correct, however, here's how to set Windows straight:

1. Open the Display Properties dialog box if it's not already open. (To do so, right-click the desktop and choose Properties.)

2. Display the Settings tab if you're not already there.

3. Click the Advanced button, and then click the Monitor tab.

4. Click the Change button.

5. Click Specify the location of the driver (Advanced) and then click Next.

6. Click Display a list of all the drivers in a specific location, so you can select the driver you want. Then click Next.

7. Click Show All Hardware.

8. Select your monitor make and model from the list that appears, and then click Next.

NOTE If your monitor doesn't appear on the list, but you have a disk that came with it, insert the disk and click the Have Disk button.

9. Click Next to move through the remainder of the Wizard until you come to the Finish button; then click Finish to install the driver for your chosen monitor.

10. Click Close to close the properties box for the video card/monitor.

11. Click OK to close the Display Properties box.

Windows now knows the correct video card and monitor, and the correct drivers are installed for them. Now you can move on to setting the video mode you want to use.

Selecting a Video Mode

Based on the video card and monitor, Windows lets you choose among several video modes. A video mode is made up of two main factors: resolution and color depth. (A third, more minor factor is refresh rate, which I cover in the next section.)

Resolution is the number of individual pixels (dots) that make up the video mode. The higher the numbers, the smaller the dots and the sharper the image (and the smaller the image). Figures 3.16 and 3.17 show the same screen at 640×480 and 1024×768 resolutions, respectively. The most common resolutions are 640×480, 800×600, and 1024×768. The first number refers to the number of pixels horizontally; the second number vertically.

Which resolution is best? It all depends on what you plan to do with your PC and the size of your monitor. As you can see by comparing Figures 3.16 and 3.17, a higher resolution makes everything look smaller. If you have a large monitor, you can use a high resolution without straining your eyes to see things. On a small monitor, you might want to stick with a lower resolution.

Figure 3.16

A typical Windows
screen at 640×480

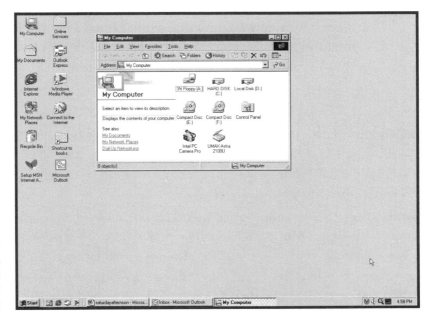

Figure 3.17

A typical Windows
screen at
1024×768

Think, too, about how you use your PC. Users who work with large spreadsheets might appreciate a higher resolution because it allows them to see more spreadsheet cells on the screen at once. But users who spend a long time sitting at the computer reading e-mail each day might find that a lower resolution prevents eyestrain because the text is larger.

Color depth is the number of colors that can be displayed simultaneously onscreen. Standard VGA is 16 colors; most people run Windows in at least 256-color mode (8-bit). High Color (16-bit) and True Color (24-bit) are higher modes that show more colors. Why is color depth important? If you display photographs or video clips onscreen, they will look much more realistic at higher color depths because of the colors shown onscreen. When you use a lower color depth, Windows attempts to simulate the missing colors by blending two or more colors in a crosshatch pattern. This is called *dithering*. From a distance it looks okay, but when you examine it closely, it looks fuzzy. When you use a higher color depth, Windows has more real colors to work with, so it doesn't have to dither as much.

In general, more color depth is better. However, if you want to use a program (usually a game) that works best at a particular color depth, you might want to temporarily set the color depth for a lower setting than the

---

COLOR BITS, RESOLUTION, AND VIDEO CARD MEMORY

The number of bits in a color depth is the number of bits of computer data required to define the color of each pixel. A bit is a single binary off/on switch, 0 for Off or 1 for On. An 8-bit number might look something like this: 01101110. There are 256 possible combinations of 0 and 1 in a string that's eight characters long, so that's why 8-bit color is the same as 256-color.

Your video card has some memory on it, and it dictates the resolution and color depth combination that you can use. For example, at 640×480 resolution, there are 307,200 individual pixels. With 8-bit color, each of them requires eight bits (that is, one byte) of memory, or approximately 307KB. The same 8-bit display at 800×600 resolution uses 480KB. Most video cards have at least 4MB of memory these days, which is more than enough to display 1024×768 with 24-bit color. (Quick quiz: how much memory is required for such a display? Answer: 2,359,296 bytes, or about 2.4MB.)

maximum your system is capable of. Such programs usually state in the documentation, onscreen during setup, or in both places that they prefer a certain color depth.

TIP Using a lower color depth, such as 256 colors, can sometimes make an older PC perform a little better because the display is less processing-intensive.

To change the video mode (both resolution and color depth), follow these steps:

1. Right-click the desktop and choose Properties.

2. Select the Settings tab.

3. Open the Colors drop-down list and choose the color depth you want.

4. Drag the Screen area slider to the resolution you want. For example, in Figure 3.18, the slider is set for 800×600.

5. Click OK.

Figure 3.18

Set the resolution (screen area) and color depth (colors).

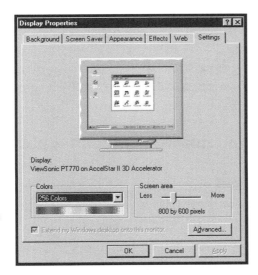

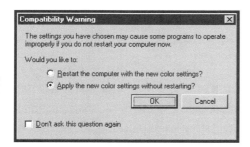

Figure 3.19

You'll see this warning when you change the color depth.

6. Do one of the following:

⚙ If you are changing the resolution only, a message appears that Windows will now resize the desktop. Click OK to acknowledge it, and then click Yes when asked whether you want to keep the new setting.

⚙ If you are changing the color depth only, or the color depth plus the resolution, a compatibility warning appears, as shown in Figure 3.19. You can choose to apply the new color settings without restarting, or you can choose to restart the computer with the new color settings. Then click OK. If you chose not to restart, click Yes when asked whether you want to keep the new settings. If you chose to restart, the computer reboots.

What's the correct answer to the compatibility warning in Figure 3.19? Well, it depends. You can try to change without restarting and it won't hurt anything, but strange things can appear on your display if you don't restart, such as missing or wrong icons. These phenomena are harmless and they fix themselves when you restart.

Changing the Display Refresh Rate

The *refresh rate* is the rate at which the image onscreen is refreshed, or repainted, by the light beams inside the monitor. The higher the refresh rate, the less flicker in the display.

If you have ever seen video footage of a computer system in which the monitor appeared to be scrolling or blinking, that was because of a refresh rate on the monitor that was out of sync with the video recording speed. The human eye doesn't notice it as much, but it's obvious on videotape. The flicker of a low refresh rate (under 72Hz) can make your eyes tired if you look at it for a long time.

Here are your choices for refresh rate:

- **Adapter default.** This is the default setting for your video card. It is not always the highest possible setting but it works with every monitor, so it's a safe setting.

- **Optimal.** This is the highest setting possible given the monitor and video card that Windows thinks you have. Windows examines the capabilities of both devices and arrives at the highest common setting they can both support.

- **Specific settings.** If this is available for your video card and monitor, you can choose a specific setting (measured in Hz). Higher is better.

❖ ❖

If the refresh rate you choose exceeds the capabilities of either your monitor or your video card, the screen will appear distorted or even scrambled. It can damage your monitor to run it at a too-high refresh rate, although this is rare.

❖ ❖

To set the refresh rate, do the following:

1. Right-click the desktop and choose Properties.

2. Click the Settings tab.

3. Click the Advanced button.

4. Click the Adapter tab.

5. Open the Refresh rate drop-down list and choose the setting you want. See Figure 3.20. If you don't know what to pick, choose Optimal.

6. Click OK. A message appears that Windows is going to adjust your refresh rate.

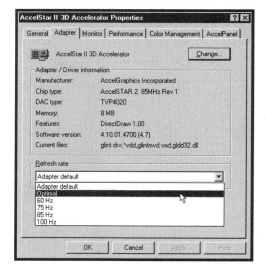

Figure 3.20

Adjust the refresh
rate on the
Adapter tab.

7. Click OK. The refresh rate changes and a message appears asking whether you want to keep the setting.

8. Click Yes.

9. Click OK to close the Display Properties dialog box.

After adjusting the refresh rate and the video mode, the image you see onscreen might be slightly off-center, slightly too large (edges cut off), or too small (a black ring around the outside) for the monitor. On most monitors you can adjust the image size and positioning with its built-in controls. See the manual that came with your monitor for details. If there are no adjustment controls, try a different refresh rate or a different monitor driver.

Working with Color Schemes

By now you might have already found the feature in Windows that allows you to change the colors of onscreen objects. Or perhaps a child in your home has found it, in which case it becomes imperative that you learn about the feature yourself so you can get rid of the awful garish colors he or she has probably selected!

Almost everything onscreen can be colorized. The Windows default colors are merely a suggestion. So, for example, you can have a purple desktop, pink title bars, and mauve dialog boxes and menus if you are so inclined.

Choosing a Color Scheme

Windows comes with a variety of color schemes, which are pre-selected color sets that look good together (or perhaps not, in your opinion!). When you are first starting out working with colors, you will probably want to apply a color scheme.

NOTE If someone has messed with your colors, you can reset them to the default colors by choosing the Windows Standard color scheme.

To choose a different color scheme:

1. Right-click the desktop and choose Properties.

2. Click the Appearance tab.

3. Open the Scheme drop-down list and choose a different color scheme.

4. Check the preview area at the top of the dialog box to see the new scheme. If desired, click the Apply button to see it applied to Windows. See Figure 3.21.

5. Repeat steps 3 and 4 as needed to find a scheme you like, and then click OK to accept it.

Some of the schemes have something in parentheses after them. Here's a key:

✿   Large means that there are custom fonts defined for the color scheme that make text on menus and in dialog boxes display larger than normal onscreen. This can be helpful for someone who is vision-impaired. Some other schemes have large text in title bars only, but these don't have the "Large" designation in their names.

✿   Extra Large is like Large, but more so.

Figure 3.21

Select a color
scheme.

○ VGA means the color scheme will look good even in regular VGA
colors (that is, 4-bit or 16 colors).

○ High Color means the color scheme will probably not look good
unless you use at least High Color (16-bit) color depth.

Customizing a Color Scheme

Once you become comfortable with the idea of color schemes, you will
probably want to customize one or more of them. You do this by picking
an individual screen element, such as desktop, title bar, or menu bar, and
then specifying a color of your choice for it (and in the case of text elements like menus, specifying a font for it).

To customize a color scheme:

1. Select a color scheme, as described in steps 1-4 of the preceding
procedure.

2. Click a part of the screen in the preview area at the top of the dialog box,
or open the Item drop-down list and choose the name of a screen item.

3. Choose a color for the item in the Color box to the right of the Item
drop-down list.

4. Some items also allow you to set their size; if the Size box is available, use its increment buttons to change the size of the item as desired. See Figure 3.22.

5. If you are working in High Color or True Color depth, the Color 2 box will be available for some items (such as title bars). This lets you set a color fade. Choose a second color if the Color 2 box is available and if desired.

6. If the item you chose contains text, the Font drop-down list will be available. Choose a font from it if desired.

7. Choose a Size and Color for the font, and click the Bold (**B**) or Italic (*I*) buttons if you want the text to be bold or italicized.

8. Go back to step 2 to choose and customize another part of the scheme as desired.

9. When you are finished customizing, save your new scheme. To do so, click the Save As button. Enter a name for your scheme, and click OK.

10. Click OK to close the Display Properties box and accept your new scheme.

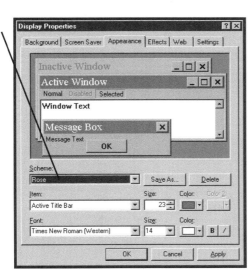

Figure 3.22

Customize individual elements of a particular scheme. Here, the active title bar is being customized.

Using Desktop Wallpaper and Patterns

You just saw how to change the desktop's color. Wallpaper and patterns are two additional ways of dressing up the desktop's appearance. *Wallpaper* places a picture on the desktop, partially or fully obscuring the chosen desktop color. A *pattern* is like a black lattice placed over the top of the background color. Figure 3.23 shows a desktop with both a wallpaper image and a pattern applied.

NOTE If you get a message that the wallpaper can be shown only if the Active Desktop is displayed, click Yes to turn that feature on. I'll explain about the Active Desktop later in the book.

Figure 3.23 shows the wallpaper centered, but you can also tile or stretch it if you prefer. Tile fills the desktop with multiple copies of the image, whereas Stretch enlarges and stretches the image (possibly distorting it) so that it exactly fills the desktop.

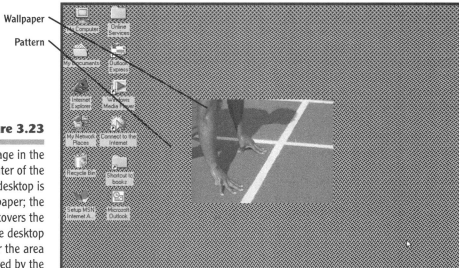

Wallpaper

Pattern

Figure 3.23

The image in the center of the desktop is wallpaper; the pattern covers the entire desktop (except for the area obscured by the wallpaper or by icons).

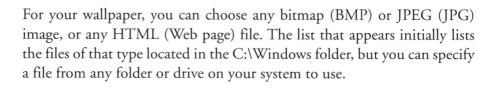

For your wallpaper, you can choose any bitmap (BMP) or JPEG (JPG) image, or any HTML (Web page) file. The list that appears initially lists the files of that type located in the C:\Windows folder, but you can specify a file from any folder or drive on your system to use.

 TIP Internet Explorer lets you save any picture you find as wallpaper. Simply right-click the picture on a Web page and choose Set as Wallpaper from the shortcut menu.

To choose a wallpaper:

1. Right-click the desktop and choose Properties.

2. Click the Background tab.

3. Select a picture from the list, or click Browse and locate the picture you want to use. See Figure 3.24.

   To remove wallpaper, choose (None) from the top of the list.

4. Open the Picture Display drop-down list and choose Center, Tile, or Stretch.

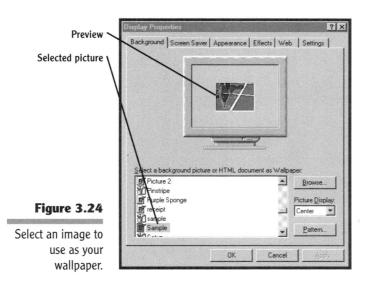

Figure 3.24

Select an image to use as your wallpaper.

5. (Optional) Click Apply to see how it's going to look on your desktop.

6. When you are happy with the chosen wallpaper settings, click OK.

And here's how to apply a pattern:

1. Follow steps 1 and 2 from the preceding procedure to open the Display Properties dialog box and display the Background tab.

2. Click the Pattern button. The Pattern dialog box opens.

3. Click a pattern, and check it out in the Preview area. See Figure 3.25.

4. (Optional) To edit the pattern, click the Edit Pattern button. The Pattern Editor window opens, shown in Figure 3.26. From here:

   A. Click individual squares in the pattern to turn the color on/off.

   B. Change the pattern name if you want to retain the original pattern as well as the new changed version.

   C. When you are done working with the pattern, click Done to return to the Pattern dialog box.

   D. If prompted to save the changes to the pattern, click Yes.

5. Click OK to accept your pattern.

6. (Optional) Click Apply to check how the pattern will look.

7. Click OK to accept your choice of pattern.

Figure 3.25

Select a pattern to use on your desktop, or choose (None) to remove the current pattern.

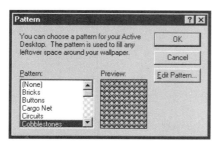

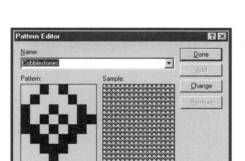

Figure 3.26

You can edit any of the existing patterns with the Pattern Editor.

Working with Screen Savers

Back in the early days of computing, if an image stayed on the screen too long, a ghost of that image was permanently "burned in" to the screen. You could see this on very old ATM machine screens, for example, and old video arcade games. Screen savers were invented to kick in after a certain period of inactivity and keep a moving image on the screen at all times to prevent this burn-in.

Nowadays monitor technology is so much better that burn-in is no longer a problem, but screen savers have gotten so creative and entertaining that people still use them anyway.

Windows comes with several screen savers to choose from. You can turn screen savers on or off, set the amount of time to elapse before the screen saver starts, and even set a password for returning to normal operation after the screen saver activates.

NOTE The password feature of Screen Savers is not very powerful. If someone is determined to get into your computer, all they need to do is press the Power or Reset button to make the computer restart. However, having a screen saver password does prevent the casual passer-by from getting too inquisitive.

To choose and control a screen saver, do the following:

1. Right-click the desktop and choose Properties.

2. Click the Screen Saver tab.

3. Open the Screen Saver drop-down list and choose a screen saver. A preview of it appears above the list. See Figure 3.27.

NOTE

If you don't have many screen savers, you might not have them all installed. Use Add/Remove programs to add the additional screen savers as you learned at the beginning of the Saturday Morning session. They're located in the Accessories category.

4. Enter the amount of delay, in minutes, in the Wait box.

5. Click the Settings button. A box appears unique to that screen saver, allowing you to customize its settings. For example, Figure 3.28 shows the settings for 3D Pipes. Make your selections and click OK.

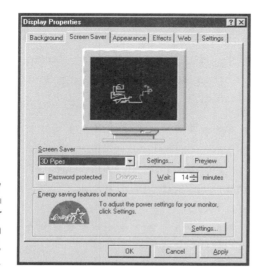

Figure 3.27

Select a screen saver to use, or to turn screen saver use off, select (None).

Figure 3.28

Each screen saver
has its own
settings.

6. (Optional) If you want to set a password to be entered when coming out of the screen saver, click the Password Protected check box and then do the following:

   A. Click the Change button.

   B. Type the password in the New Password box.

   C. Type it again in the Confirm New Password box.

   D. Click OK.

7. (Optional) Click Preview to see the screen saver in action. Moving your mouse or pressing any key will exit the screen saver preview.

8. Click OK to close the Display Properties and accept the screen saver.

Changing the Way Windows Acts

Now that you know how to change your display options in Windows, how about looking at some settings that affect the way Windows acts, too? These settings run the gamut from mouse pointer shape to sound effects to the number of clicks it takes to open a file. You'll be amazed! (Well okay, maybe not amazed, but would you settle for mildly entertained?)

Setting CD Auto Insert Notification

Here's a setting I mentioned back in the Friday Evening session. When you insert a CD-ROM in your drive, something happens automatically, such as a Setup program running or an audio CD playing in Media Player, if Auto insert notification is turned on for the drive. It's turned on by default.

To turn Auto insert notification on or off for a CD-ROM drive, follow these steps:

1. Open the System Properties box. To do so, right-click My Computer and choose Properties, or double-click the System icon in the Control Panel.

2. Click the Device Manager tab.

3. Click the plus sign next to CD-ROM, and then double-click your CD-ROM drive's name. Its Properties box opens.

4. Click the Settings tab.

5. Select or deselect the Auto insert notification check box. See Figure 3.29.

6. Click OK.

If you insert a CD-ROM and nothing happens, even with Auto insert notification on, perhaps that particular disk doesn't have the right files to be able to auto run. In order to auto run, it needs to either 1) be an audio CD, or 2) contain the file autorun.inf in the top-level folder. Autorun.inf contains instructions that tell Windows what program to automatically launch, such as a setup program.

Figure 3.29

Control a CD-ROM drive's Auto insert notification setting here.

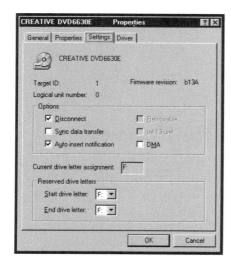

Changing File Options

Over the years, Microsoft has introduced some "improvements" to how Windows handles files. I use the term improvements in quotation marks because not everyone agrees that these changes were for the better. Some people have found them downright annoying. One such change, for example, is the personalized menu system that I showed you in the Friday Evening session.

So to make everyone happy, Microsoft has included settings in Windows that allow users to decide how they want Windows to operate regarding these improvements. In the following sections I'll show you what each of them are, and how to turn them on or off.

NOTE   In different versions of Windows, different file-management options were turned on by default. If you are working with an earlier version of Windows than Me and it's not behaving the way you expect, check to see whether some of these options are enabled or disabled.

All the options I'll tell you about in the following sections are set from the Folder Options dialog box. From any My Computer or Windows Explorer window, choose Tools, Folder Options. The first options I'll describe are on the General tab, shown in Figure 3.30; the remainder are on the View tab.

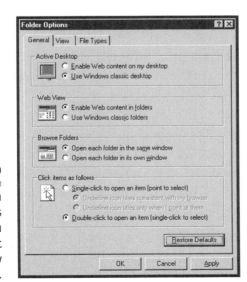

Figure 3.30

The General tab in the Folder Options dialog box lets you set some basic options for how Windows behaves.

Active Desktop

The Active Desktop is Microsoft's vision for turning the Windows interface into a giant Web page. The Active Desktop enables you to place Web content directly on your desktop, and update it continuously from the Internet. For example, you can use your favorite Web page as wallpaper or place a stock ticker on the desktop.

The Active Desktop is turned off by default, but you'll need to turn it on if you want to use desktop wallpaper (described earlier in this chapter). There are a few other Windows features that require it to be turned on as well; when you try to activate one of those features, you'll see a message letting you know and offering to turn on the Active Desktop automatically.

You can turn on the Active Desktop from the Folder Options box (Figure 3.30) by choosing Enable Web content on my desktop. Another way is to right-click the desktop and choose Active Desktop, Enable Web Content.

You probably will not notice much difference, if any, after turning on the Active Desktop. You will simply be able to use certain other Windows features, such as Active Controls and wallpaper, that you could not use before.

Active Controls are Web objects, such as HTML pages, stock tickers, jukeboxes, weather maps, and so on, that you can download from Microsoft's Web site for free and place on your desktop. To explore them, check out the Web tab in the Display Properties dialog box. (Right-click the desktop and choose Properties and then click the Web tab, or right-click the desktop and choose Active Desktop, Customize My Desktop.) From there, click the New button to visit the Web page from which you can download them.

Web View

By default, Web content is enabled in folders. That's what gives you that extra area to the left of a file listing that provides information about the selected file, folder, or drive, and that's what lets you customize the look of a folder (with the View, Customize This Folder command).

If you choose Use Windows Classic Folders instead, your folder windows will look just like they did in earlier versions of Windows (like Windows 95 for example). Figure 3.31 shows the difference. The folder on the top has Web Content enabled; the folder on the bottom does not.

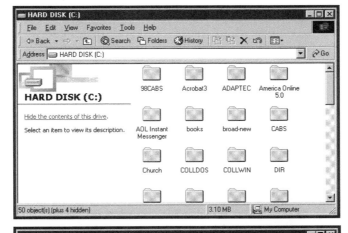

Figure 3.31

On the top,
Web Content
Enabled; on the
bottom, Windows
Classic Folders.

Browsing Folders

When you double-click a folder or drive in My Computer, that drive or folder's content appears. By default it appears in the same window, replacing the earlier contents. However, in Windows 95 it worked differently; it opened a separate window for the new content.

The default is to use the same window, but you can choose Open Each Folder in its Own Window (from the Folder Option dialog box) if you prefer.

Click Versus Double-Click

Windows 98 Second Edition came with a radical new feature: by default, the desktop and all folder windows worked like Web pages. In other words, you pointed at something to select it and single-clicked it to activate it. This was a giant step forward in making Windows integrated with the Web.

Unfortunately, most people hated it. Everyone had gotten used to the old way of doing things in Windows (single-click to select, double-click to activate), and the new method was strange and unwelcome.

So in Windows Me, Microsoft has gone back to the old way as the default. However, you can still experiment with this single-click action by choosing it from the Folder Options box. Simply select the Single Click to Open an Item (Point to Select) check box. You can further choose to underline items all the time or only when they are pointed at. Figure 3.32 shows Windows with this single-click method active and items set to be underlined full-time.

 **CAUTION**

If you turn on the single-click method, most of the procedures described in this book won't work exactly as written; you'll need to modify them to single-click instead of double-click and point instead of single-click.

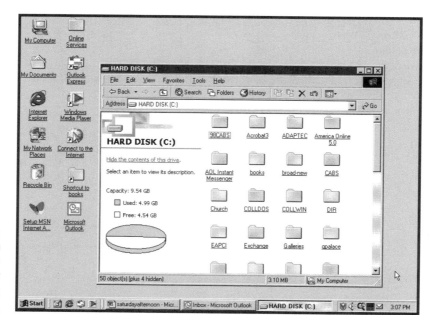

Figure 3.32

The Windows desktop set up for single-click operation.

Showing File Extensions

You might have noticed in Friday Evening's session that some files show their file extensions and others don't. A file extension is a code that comes after the file name (with a period in-between). It tells Windows what kind of file it is. By default, Windows hides the file extensions for file types that it recognizes, and shows the file extensions for types that it doesn't recognize.

As you move past the beginner level in Windows, you might want to see all file extensions, to give yourself more control over your file listings. For example, you might have two files in the same folder, both called Booklet, but one of them is Booklet.xls and the other is Booklet.doc. Windows recognizes both .xls and .doc extensions, so it shows both files as simply "Booklet" in file listings. You can tell the files apart by looking at their differing icons, but you can't be sure what their exact extensions are. If file extensions were turned on, however, it would be a simpler matter.

You turn on file extensions from the View tab of the Folder Options dialog box:

1. If the Folder Options dialog box is not already open, choose Tools, Folder Options from any file listing window.

2. Click the View tab. See Figure 3.33.

Figure 3.33

The View tab contains lots more file options, including the capability to show or hide extensions for known file types.

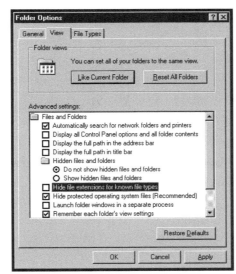

3. Scroll through the Advanced Settings list and deselect the Hide file extensions for known file types check box.

4. Click OK.

Other Advanced File Options

At this point you might be curious about those other items on the Advanced Settings list. Most of them you will probably never need, but to satisfy your curiosity, Table 3.2 describes them.

Keyboard Settings

For most people, the keyboard is the primary way of entering data into Windows. So it's important that it works in a comfortable way for you.

To adjust your keyboard settings, double-click the Keyboard icon in the Control Panel. This opens the Keyboard Properties box shown in Figure 3.34.

There are three settings. Two of them have to do with character repeat. That's where you hold down a key and, after a second or two, it starts repeating quickly on your screen. You can use it to create a whole row of a certain character, such as a dash or dot, very quickly.

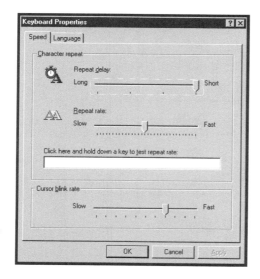

Figure 3.34

Change keyboard properties here.

TABLE 3.2 ADVANCED FILE OPTIONS	
Option	**Purpose**
Automatically search for network folders and printers	Instructs Windows to periodically search the network for shared drives, folders, and printers, and adds them to My Network Places.
Display all Control Panel options and all folder contents	Shows the full listing of Control Panel options and the full contents of certain important folders such as Windows. By default this is turned off, to keep beginners out of trouble.
Display the full path in the address bar	When viewing a folder, that folder's full path appears in the address bar, as opposed to just the name of the folder.
Display the full path in title bar	Same thing as above except applies to the window's title bar.
Hidden files and folders	Enables you to choose whether file listings include files marked as hidden. If you show hidden files, they appear with their icons "ghosted" to let you know they are hidden files.
Hide file extensions for known file types	You already learned about this one in the preceding section.
Hide protected operating system files	Excludes files from file listings that are essential for computer startup and Windows operation.
Launch folder windows in a separate process	Opens separate folder windows in a separate part of memory in Windows; minimizes the damage from program errors, but uses more memory.
Remember each folder's view settings	Saves the choices you make when viewing a folder, such as icon size and file arrangement, and uses the same settings the next time you open that folder.
Show My Documents on the desktop	Displays or hides the My Documents folder on the desktop. You can get to it through its full path, C:\Windows\My Documents, if not from the desktop.
Show pop-up description for folder and desktop items	Shows or hides ScreenTips that pop up when you point at certain folders and icons.

The settings are:

🔧 **Repeat delay.** The amount of time between when you start holding down a key and when character repeat kicks in.

🔧 **Character repeat.** The speed at which characters repeat after the character repeat feature starts.

🔧 **Cursor blink rate.** The speed at which the insertion point blinks when it is in a text box and ready to accept typing.

You can set the repeat delay and the character repeat by dragging the respective slider bars, and then test your new setting in the text box provided.

The other tab in the Keyboard Properties dialog box, Language, is rather specialized, and you won't need it if you use only one language with Windows. If you buy language packs that allow Windows to support other language keyboards, you can switch between keyboards using the settings on the Language tab.

Mouse Settings

There are a lot more mouse settings than keyboard settings! You can control the look of the onscreen mouse pointers, the speed at which the pointer moves across the screen, and more.

NOTE If you have some special kind of mouse, such as a fancy trackball, it might have come with its own software. If so, and if that software is installed, your mouse properties won't look like the ones shown here. Refer to the documentation for that device instead.

Buttons

The Buttons tab in the Mouse Properties dialog box gives you three settings to control:

🔧 **Button configuration.** Sets which mouse button does what. If you are left-handed, for example, you might want to switch the functions

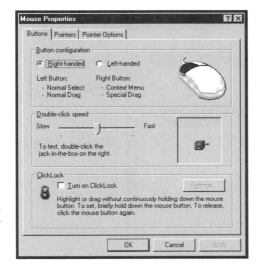

Figure 3.35

Set options for your
mouse buttons on
the Buttons tab.

of the right and left mouse buttons so that your strong finger (your
index finger) rests on the button you'll use the most when the mouse
is in your left hand.

- **Double-click speed.** Sets the minimum speed that you must double-
  click in order for Windows to recognize it as such, rather than as two
  single-clicks. Drag the slider bar to adjust it and then double-click
  the jack-in-the-box picture to test your setting. See Figure 3.35.

- **Turn on ClickLock.** Turns on an Accessibility feature that is helpful
  to some people with disabilities. When ClickLock is on, you can
  briefly hold down the mouse button to "lock" the button down, and
  then do the same again to release it. It's kind of like the Caps Lock
  on your keyboard.

Pointers

You might have noticed that the mouse pointer takes on different shapes
when you do different things in Windows. For example, while you're waiting it looks like an hourglass, and while you're hovering over a text box it
becomes a curly capital-I (an "I-beam").

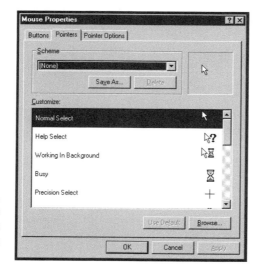

Figure 3.36

Choose how the pointers look on the Pointers tab.

Each of those little pointer images is controlled by the setting on the Pointers tab. You can define pictures for individual pointers, or choose a whole set of pointers as a group (a *pointer scheme*).

To change an individual pointer:

1. Click the pointer type to customize from the Customize list. See Figure 3.36.

2. Click the Browse button.

3. Select the pointer you want to use instead.

4. Click OK.

To change the entire pointer scheme, open the Scheme drop-down list and choose the one you want. For example, those who have difficulty seeing the pointer onscreen might want to use the Windows Standard (Extra Large) pointer scheme.

NOTE When you apply a desktop theme, covered later in this chapter, you also get custom mouse pointers that go along with the chosen scheme.

Pointer Options

The Pointer Options tab contains settings that deal with the pointer's appearance and movement on the screen. Here's what you have to choose from:

- **Pointer Speed.** Drag the slider to adjust the sensitivity of the pointer movement onscreen in relation to your mouse movement.

- **SnapTo.** Turn this on if you want the pointer to automatically jump to the default button in a dialog box (such as OK).

- **Show Pointer Trails.** Turn this on to see trails (kind of like the white trail that an airplane leaves across the sky) behind the mouse as it moves. Try it out, but you'll probably find it annoying pretty soon. It's primarily for those with visual impairments that make it difficult for them to find the pointer onscreen.

- **Hide Pointer While Typing.** Turn this on to make the pointer disappear when you are typing, and reappear when you stop.

- **Show Location of Pointer When You Press the Ctrl Key.** Just what the name says. It helps you find the pointer onscreen if you have trouble seeing it.

Regional Settings

The Regional Settings, accessible from the Control Panel, control the country-specific standards such as the default currency symbol, the date and time format, and the number format, and digit grouping.

By default, Windows is set up for United States (English) settings, but if you are in another country, or work primarily with those in another country, you might want to experiment with these settings.

1. Choose Start, Settings, Control Panel.

2. Double-click Regional Settings.

3. Do one of the following:

   - Select the language and country from the Language and Country/Region drop-down lists on the Regional Settings tab. This automatically sets all other settings on the other tabs.

Figure 3.37

Choose settings for
numbers, currency,
and dates and
times, or simply
choose a country
from the Regional
Settings tab to take
care of all settings
at once.

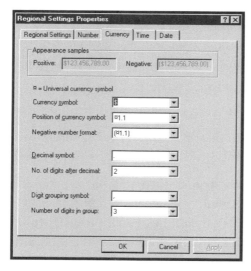

* Go to each tab individually (Number, Currency, Date, and Time) and make individual setting choices. For example, Figure 3.37 shows the Currency tab.

4. Click OK.

Sound Schemes

If you have a sound card and speakers, Windows probably makes noise. You might hear a ding or beep, for example, when an error message appears onscreen or when you receive new mail in your e-mail program. There might also be little tunes that play when you start up or shut down.

All these sounds and songs are controlled by the Sounds and Multimedia settings in Windows. You can choose individual sound files (in WAV format) to be associated with specific system events, such as Shutdown, or you can apply a sound scheme that assigns a predefined set of sounds to a whole list of system events at once.

To control the sounds that Windows makes, follow these steps:

1. Choose Start, Settings, Control Panel.

2. Double-click Sounds and Multimedia.

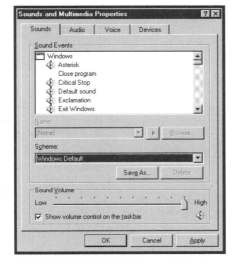

Figure 3.38

Choose a sound scheme, or assign individual WAV files to system events.

3. Click the Sounds tab if it is not already on top. See Figure 3.38.

4. Click a sound event on the list, and then click the Play button to hear it. Do this for each of the events that interest you.

5. (Optional) Open the Scheme drop-down list and choose a different sound scheme.

● ●

NOTE   If there is only one sound scheme on the list (Windows Default), you can install additional sound schemes using Add/Remove Programs in the Control Panel. You'll find them in the Multimedia group of Windows components. See Saturday Morning's session to learn about adding Windows components and accessories.

● ●

6. (Optional) To customize an individual event, click the event on the list, and then choose a sound for it from the Name drop-down list. Or click the Browse button and select another sound file located elsewhere on your PC to serve as the sound for that event. Repeat this for each sound event you want to customize. You can click the Play button to test any of the sounds.

7. (Optional) To save your sound settings in a new scheme, click the Save As button. Enter a name for the new scheme, and click OK.

8. (Optional) Adjust the sound volume by dragging the Volume slider at the bottom of the dialog box.

9. Click OK to accept your new settings.

Applying Desktop Themes

Desktop themes are like color schemes on steroids. They're collections of colors, wallpaper, mouse pointers, sounds, screen savers, and more, all centered around a particular theme. So far in this chapter you have learned how to choose each of those items independently of one another; now you'll learn how to apply a whole set at once.

To apply a desktop theme:

1. Choose Start, Settings, Control Panel.

2. Double-click Desktop Themes. The Desktop Themes dialog box opens.

   If you don't see Desktop Themes in the control panel, the feature is not installed; add it as you learned at the beginning of the Saturday Morning session.

3. (Optional) If you want to save your current settings as a scheme before applying a different one, click Save As. Enter a name for the scheme, and click Save.

   That way you can always return to your current settings later if desired. You can also remove the current scheme later by choosing Windows Default as the theme.

4. Open the Theme drop-down list and choose a theme to examine. A preview of it appears. See Figure 3.39.

5. (Optional) To preview the screen saver, click the Screen Saver button. Move the mouse or press any key to return.

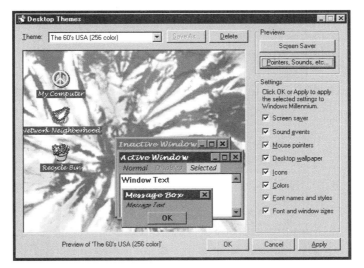

Figure 3.39

Set up desktop themes here.

6. (Optional) To preview the pointers, sounds, and other elements that aren't shown on the preview, click the Pointers, Sounds, etc. button. A Preview dialog box appears, shown in Figure 3.40. Use the settings in this box to preview the pointers, sounds, and visuals (that is, the icons on your desktop); then click Close to return.

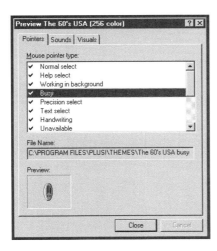

Figure 3.40

Preview the sounds and pointers here.

TIP ■
More themes are available at http://www.tucows.com.
■ ■

7. To decline to use one of the elements of the scheme, deselect its
    check box, and the previous settings for that item will be used.

    For example, to keep your existing sounds rather than applying the
    sounds that come with the scheme, deselect Sound Events.

8. Click OK to accept the scheme and close the dialog box.

To remove a theme, you can return to the Desktop Themes dialog box later
and choose Windows Default or Windows Me as the theme. This returns
you to the default settings in all categories.

Wrapping Up

Now that you've got Windows working just the way you want it, take a
dinner break! In this evening's session, you'll use your computer as a launching pad for exploring the Internet.

Improving System Performance

- Checking the System for Errors with ScanDisk
- Defragmenting the Hard Disk
- Setting Cache Size
- Updating Your System
- Deleting Unwanted Files and Programs
- Scheduling Maintenance Tasks

By now your Windows system is looking pretty good, right? You know what the big pieces are for, and you've probably got some snazzy colors, sounds, and pointers going on too. This evening's session takes customization one step beyond by helping you tune up your PC to top performance.

None of these activities will turn an old clunker into a powerhouse PC, but they can result in a modest speedup in your everyday work and some small but noticeable usability improvements.

Checking the System for Errors with ScanDisk

ScanDisk is probably the single most useful Windows utility you will learn about in this entire book. Running ScanDisk can often do wonders to fix problems, such as random Windows lockups and sluggish performance.

When Windows appears to be malfunctioning, it's often because of a disk error. There are two kinds of disk errors: physical and logical. ScanDisk corrects both kinds.

A *physical error* on a disk is a "bad spot" from which data cannot be read. Physical errors are usually caused by physical trauma to the computer, such as falling off a table while it is running.

A *logical error* on a disk is because of a problem with the disk's "table of contents" called the *File Allocation Table* (FAT). Logical errors are often caused by shutting off the computer's power while it is running or by a program locking up and failing to close its files properly. Logical errors can snowball if not corrected; one program might lock up because of an existing error and in turn generate even more errors. Even when you don't see an error message onscreen, a problem can still exist that ScanDisk can correct.

Of the two types, logical errors are far more common. You can run two types of checks with ScanDisk: Standard and Thorough. Standard checks only for logical errors and takes only a few minutes; Thorough checks for both and takes a lot longer to run, up to several hours.

NOTE Most people do not run the Thorough check unless they suspect a physical problem. If you recently knocked the PC off a table, for example, you might want to run a Thorough check. You might also suspect physical problems if you see an error message including the words "data error reading" or "data error writing."

To run ScanDisk, close all running applications, and then follow these steps:

1. Choose Start, Programs, Accessories, System Tools, ScanDisk. The ScanDisk program starts and a list of drives appears.

2. Click the drive you want to check. If you want to check more then one drive, hold down the Ctrl key while you click multiple drive letters. See Figure 4.1.

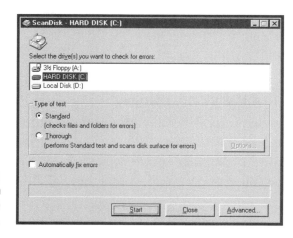

Figure 4.1

Select the drive to check for errors.

3. Click Thorough to run the full test, or leave Standard selected to check only for logical errors. Thorough can take several hours, so you probably won't want to use it every time.

4. Select the Automatically fix errors check box to avoid having to deal with the errors it finds (especially if you're a beginner).

5. Click Start.

6. Wait for the checking to finish. A Standard test takes less than five minutes; a Thorough test can take several hours, depending on the size of your hard disk.

   A message box reports ScanDisk's findings when it is finished.

7. Click Close to close the message box. Then click Close in the ScanDisk window to close the program.

NOTE

ScanDisk restarts whenever the disk content changes, so don't do anything on your PC while ScanDisk is running. If it continually restarts and isn't able to finish even though you aren't touching it, perhaps a program running in the background is interfering. Try closing all running programs except System Tray and Explorer. To do so, press Ctrl+Alt+Delete, and then click a program to close and choose End Task.

If you have Microsoft Office installed, a program called Find Fast is probably operating in the background. To pause it, go to the Control Panel and double-click Find Fast. Then choose Index, Pause Indexing.

Defragmenting the Hard Disk

To understand fragmentation and defragmenting, you need to know something about how files are stored on disk.

The storage system on a hard disk is not sequential. For example, suppose you have a word processing document that takes up 18 clusters (that is, organizational units) on the hard disk. Those clusters are not necessarily adjacent to one another; they might be scattered all over the disk. The File Allocation

Table (FAT) keeps a record of which 18 clusters that file uses, and when you open the file, the disk's read/write head hops around gathering up the pieces so they can be assembled into a whole file in your word processor.

When a file is not stored in all-adjacent clusters, it's considered a fragmented file. As you can imagine, hopping all over the disk to pick up the fragments takes time, which is why fragmentation slows down your system performance.

How does fragmentation happen in the first place? Well, when your hard disk is empty, files are written to it in sequential clusters. Suppose, for example, you save a spreadsheet files that uses five clusters. Then perhaps you install another program. The new files are written right next to your spreadsheet file. Now, you reopen the spreadsheet file and enter more data into it, and it ends up needing a total of nine clusters. No clusters are available next to the original five, so the additional four clusters' worth of data must go somewhere else. Now the file is fragmented. Over time, your file can be split into many fragments all over the disk.

When you defragment, a special program rearranges the content of your hard disk so that all files are stored in sequential clusters. That way, when you open the files the disk read/write head reads from a single spot rather than having to hop around, so it can read faster.

Therefore, for best performance, you should defragment your disk regularly (for example, once a month).

To run the Disk Defragmenter, follow these steps:

1. Choose Start, Programs, Accessories, System Tools, Disk Defragmenter. The Select Drive dialog box asks which drive you want to defragment. You can defragment only one drive at a time.

 NOTE You can defragment a floppy disk or other removable disk, but it's probably not worth the trouble. Most likely you will not open files from such disks very often.

2. Select your hard disk from the list, and then click OK. (If you have more than one hard disk, you will need to repeat the process starting here at step 2 for each drive.)

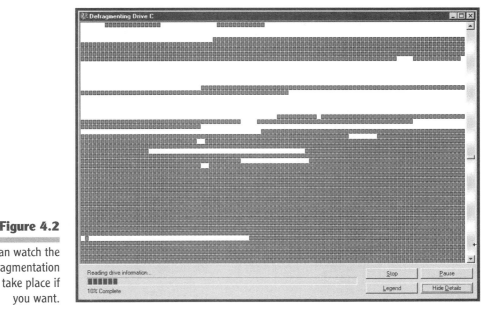

Figure 4.2

You can watch the
defragmentation
take place if
you want.

3. Click OK to start the defragmentation process. Then wait for the drive to be defragmented.

   To entertain yourself while you're waiting, click Show Details to watch a graphical representation of the proceedings, as shown in Figure 4.2.

4. When it finishes, the program asks if you want to quit. Click Yes, or click No and go back to step 2.

Setting Cache Size

Caches are blocks of memory set aside to temporarily store data the processor has just used and might need again soon. Using a cache makes your PC run faster because memory access is much faster than disk access.

Buffers are related to caches. A buffer is a holding area in memory for data waiting to be processed or sent to an output device. For example, when you print, the print job waits in a print buffer for the printer to print it. Also, when you create a CD-ROM with a writable CD drive, if the PC sends data to the drive faster than it can write it, the excess data waits in the drive's buffer until it can be written.

Both your hard disk and your CD-ROM drive employ cache/buffering systems. You can sometimes slightly improve the performance of a drive by increasing its cache setting. (You can always decrease that setting again later if the larger setting causes problems.)

To check and change drive cache settings, follow these steps:

1. Right-click My Computer on the desktop and choose Properties.

2. Select the Performance tab in the System Properties dialog box.

3. Click File System. The File System Properties dialog box opens.

4. On the Hard Disk tab (see Figure 4.3), open the Typical role of this computer drop-down list and choose Network server. This increases the buffer size, speeding up disk access slightly. (It doesn't matter that your PC isn't a network server.)

5. Make sure the Read-ahead optimization slider is set to Full (all the way to the right).

6. Select the CD-ROM tab.

7. Make sure the Supplemental cache size slider is set to Large (all the way to the right), as shown in Figure 4.4.

Figure 4.3

Choose Network server for the typical role of the computer.

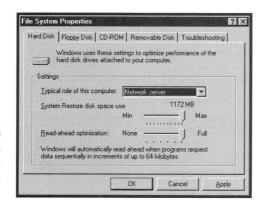

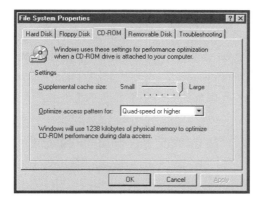

Figure 4.4

Set performance
properties for
the CD-ROM
drive here.

8. Make sure the Optimize access pattern for drop-down list is set to Quad-speed or higher.

9. If you have any removable drives (such as Zip drives), click the Removable Disk tab. (Skip to step 11 if you do not.)

10. Make sure the Enable Write-behind Caching on All Removable Disk Drives check box is marked.

11. Click OK.

12. Click Close to close the File System Properties dialog box.

13. If you see a message that says you must restart your computer, click Yes to do so.

Controlling Which Programs Load at Startup

Lots of programs load when Windows starts, and you might not even be aware of them. For example, if you have an antivirus program, it loads at startup. If you have a fax device, a rewritable CD-ROM drive, a scanner, or other special hardware, each of these devices might also load its own behind-the-scenes program at startup.

The fewer programs that load at startup, the more Windows resources are left for other activities. So for best performance, make sure there are no programs loading automatically at startup that you don't need.

NOTE Another way to control what programs load at startup is through the Custom setup for the Maintenance Wizard, covered in the section entitled "Running the Maintenance Wizard," near the end of this chapter.

Finding Out What Programs Are Loaded

Just what all is really running? To find out, press Ctrl+Alt+Delete right after you start Windows. The Close Program dialog box appears, listing all the running programs. You might be surprised at the long list! Each open window and each running program is represented there. When you are done looking, click Close to cancel this dialog box. (It's not a good idea to close a running program from this dialog box unless it is malfunctioning and can't be closed normally.)

Don't worry if you don't recognize the cryptic names of the running programs; you don't need to know what every one of them does. Displaying this list is just an exercise to give you an idea of the kinds of programs that load and run automatically on your PC.

Disabling Programs in the System Tray

Some programs that load at startup place icons for themselves in your system tray, so you can control them. The system tray is the area to the left of the clock in the lower-right corner of the screen. You can right-click any of these icons to see a shortcut menu of commands that let you work with the running program.

Perhaps you just need to disable the program temporarily. You might be able to do so from the system tray. Some of these programs include a Close or Exit command on this shortcut menu, as shown in Figure 4.5, so you can unload the program when needed. For example, some installation programs for other software require that you disable your antivirus program before running them. However, the next time you start your PC, the program reloads again.

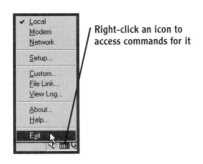

Figure 4.5

Each icon in the
system tray
represents a
program running in
the background.

Right-click an icon to
access commands for it

When you exit certain programs in the system tray, they offer to disable themselves from starting automatically in the future. This is certainly the easiest way to prevent a program from starting, if the program offers that. However, most don't offer this option.

Other programs provide a means of disabling them through their Properties, or through their main operational screen. Right-click an icon and choose its Properties command (or Options, or Configure, or some other wording; it depends on the program) from the shortcut menu; look for a check box that disables the program from starting automatically.

If the program doesn't provide a way for you to disable it, you might need to formally uninstall it to prevent it from loading at startup (assuming it's important to you that it be disabled; if it doesn't appear to be hurting anything, you might just leave it alone). See "Uninstalling Unwanted Programs" later in this chapter for help. Or, you might be able to disable it in one of the ways covered in the following sections.

Disabling Startup Programs from the StartUp Group

Some programs load at startup because shortcuts to them appear in the StartUp program group. To see these, choose Start, Programs, StartUp.

If you want to prevent any of those programs from starting automatically, simply remove them from that submenu. Right-click one and choose Delete. Deleting the shortcut from the StartUp group does not delete or disable the program itself; you can run it manually any time you need it.

For example, if you seldom use your fax software, you might remove it from the StartUp group and then run it from the Start menu to turn it on when needed.

Disabling Startup Programs with MSCONFIG

Now you're getting into the serious hunting season! If you are trying to track down a pesky unwanted program that loads at startup, and it's not in the StartUp program group, where is it being called from? Probably the Windows Registry. The Registry is a giant configuration file that Windows processes at startup, telling it what to load, what settings to use, and so on.

Windows comes with a utility program called regedit.exe (found in the C:\Windows folder) that you can use to edit the Registry, but I don't recommend that beginners (or even intermediates) do so. There is too much potential for error and for screwing up your system to the point where it won't start at all. Instead, whenever possible, I use the System Configuration Utility (a.k.a. MSCONFIG), which edits the Registry, as well as other startup files, on your behalf.

To learn how to use it, follow these steps:

1. Choose Start, Run. Type **MSCONFIG** and press Enter.

2. Click the Startup tab. A list of all the drivers and programs that load at startup appears. See Figure 4.6.

3. Remove the check mark next to any items that you don't want to execute at startup. Don't remove anything that you don't recognize; it might be something important.

4. Click OK.

5. Restart the computer.

You can also disable some other fairly techie items from the System Configuration Utility, but leave that to the experts and move on.

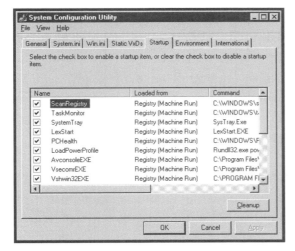

Figure 4.6

Disable certain startup programs and drivers here.

Take a Break

You're doing great. Take a quick break now, and admire the work you've done so far in this session! Your computer is probably running more nimbly and efficiently than ever. Then move on to the next section, where you'll learn about keeping your Windows installation current.

Updating Your System

Generally speaking, your system will work best when you have the latest versions of everything—of Windows, of each application, of each device driver, and so on. If your system is more than six months old, you probably do not have the latest of everything. That's fine in most cases, but if you notice problems with a particular device, the first line of troubleshooting defense is often to find a newer driver for it. In the following sections you'll learn about keeping your Windows programs and device drivers current.

Downloading Updated Drivers and Software

Hardware companies periodically release updates and improvements for their devices' Windows drivers. These updates don't just fix problems, but in some cases actually make the device work better or have additional capabilities.

The same goes for software. Depending on the program, you might be able to download a patch that fixes a specific problem or even a whole new version with new features.

You can download and install updates from the company's Web site on the Internet, or you can request that the company send you the latest drivers on a disk. (The latter might cost a small amount for postage.) Refer to the Sunday Morning session for help with the Internet.

Updating Windows with Windows Update

Windows 98, Windows 2000, and Windows Me come with a Windows Update feature that helps you keep your copy of Windows current. It connects you to a special Web site, examines your current system, and recommends downloads to you. Then, with a few clicks of the mouse, you can download and automatically install those updates.

To use Windows Update, close all open applications, and then do the following:

1. Choose Start, Windows Update. Internet Explorer (IE) opens, connects to the Internet, and displays the Windows Update screen.

2. Click the Product Updates hyperlink.

3. If asked whether it is okay for Windows to examine your system, click Yes. You might not see this.

4. A list of updates available for your system appears. Place a check mark beside each item in the Critical Updates section, plus any updates you want in the other sections. See Figure 4.7.

 NOTE A critical update is one that affects your system's security or performance in an important way. All other updates are just feature enhancements or patches to fix specialized problems.

5. Click Download. A page appears to confirm your selections.

6. Click Start Download. A license agreement appears.

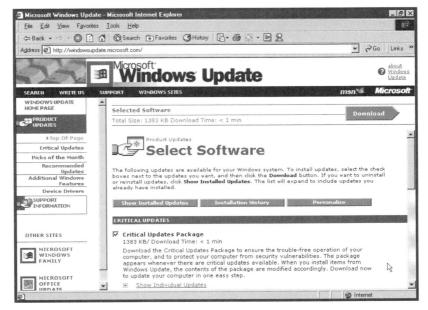

Figure 4.7

Select the updates you want. Make sure you include all critical updates.

7. Click Yes to accept the license agreement.

8. Wait for the downloads to complete and the updates to install themselves.

If you see a message that you must restart Windows, click Yes. If you don't see such a message, you merely see a Web page indicating the installation was successful, and you can close the Web browser or continue using the Internet.

 TIP   You can minimize the IE window and continue using your PC while the download completes.

Using AutoUpdate

Windows Me has a new feature called AutoUpdate that reminds you when new updates are available. When there is an update, the AutoUpdate icon appears in your taskbar, with a little balloon over it saying that an update is available. Click the balloon to open the AutoUpdate window.

The first time you use AutoUpdate, a licensing agreement appears. Click I Accept the Agreement, and then Next to continue. You'll see this only the first time.

If you see a notice about Internet connection sharing, just click Next to move past it. Then click Finish to complete the AutoUpdate setup.

Then, in the future, when AutoUpdates arrive a similar little balloon and icon in the System Tray will alert you. You simply click the icon and follow the prompts to install the update.

Uninstalling Unwanted Programs

Most people have several programs on their PCs that they never use. These programs can be uninstalled to free up disk space (often a considerable amount of it!). For example, suppose your computer came with a whole slew of programs and you have never used any of them. Getting rid of them potentially can save hundreds of megabytes of disk space. Or suppose you downloaded and installed a game demo, but the demo period has expired. It too can be axed in the interest of disk space.

Deleting a program's files through Windows Explorer or My Computer is not the preferred method. True, you are freeing up disk space, but in a rough, ungraceful way. The Windows Registry still retains information about the program being installed, and some other startup files might continue to refer to it. And, unless you are a real tech expert, you probably cannot manually remove all references to the deleted program from your system files.

A much better way is to use the Uninstall feature in Windows through Add/Remove Programs. You learned about this in Friday Evening's session, so I'll refer you there now (see the section "Removing a Program") rather than repeat the whole procedure.

Removing Windows Components

In Saturday Morning's session, you learned how to add and remove the accessory programs that come with Windows. If you are short on hard disk space, you might want to revisit that procedure now with an eye toward removing any programs that you don't use. See "Adding and Removing Accessories" at the beginning of Saturday Morning's session.

Deleting Unwanted Files

Besides removing whole programs, you can also remove individual files. One way is to select the files in Windows Explorer or My Computer and then press the Delete key. However, you shouldn't do this unless you are sure of the worthlessness of the files you are deleting, because you can screw up your system if you delete important system files.

Generally speaking, you can safely delete any data files you created yourself. You can distinguish data files from program files by their extensions (that is, the characters following the period in the name). You learned how to turn on the display of file extensions Saturday afternoon. Tables 4.1 and 4.2 list some common extensions.

Tables 4.1 and 4.2 provide only a partial list; there are many other file extensions for both programs and data files that you can encounter. If in doubt about a file, do not delete it.

TABLE 4.1 DO NOT DELETE FILES WITH THESE EXTENSIONS	
Extensions	**Used For**
.exe, .com, .bat	Programs
.dll, .bin, .dat, .ocx	Helper files for programs
.sys, .ini, .inf	Configuration or system files

TABLE 4.2 YOU CAN SAFELY DELETE FILES WITH THESE EXTENSIONS	
Extensions	**Used For**
.doc, .wpd, .wri	Word processing documents
.txt	Text files
.123, .xls, .wks	Spreadsheets
.pcx, .jpg, .bmp, .gif	Graphics
.zip, .arc, .sit, .zoo	Compressed archives
.qif, .mny, .qbk	Financial data

◆ ◆

 **CAUTION** Not all graphic files are safe to delete. Some programs (mostly games) require graphic files to run properly. If you delete the graphic files associated with the program, the program won't work. To be safe, delete only graphics you created yourself or down-loaded from the Internet.

The same goes for compressed archives. A few commercial programs (again, mostly games) use .zip files as they run; if you delete the .zip files from that program's folder, it might not work. To be safe, delete only compressed archives you downloaded from the Internet yourself.

◆ ◆

If you are not sure about the content of a particular data file, try double-clicking it. If the program that created it is still installed on your PC, the data file might open in that program and you can see what it contains.

Removing Unnecessary Files with Disk Cleanup

In addition to the data files on your hard disk, there are probably many other files that can be deleted too—if you can only locate and identify them. It's tricky for a beginner to do so reliably, though, and a single mistake can render the system inoperable.

That's where Disk Cleanup comes in handy. It looks at the files on your system and suggests files to delete in several categories. These categories include the following:

- **Temporary files.** Files that Windows or some other program created temporarily and apparently forgot to delete for some reason (such as during an abnormal shutdown). These sometimes, but not always, have a .tmp extension or the first character is a tilde (~).

- **Saved Web pages.** For faster operation, your Web browser retains information about Web pages you visit so it can display the pages more quickly if you call for them again. These saved pages can be removed safely from your system to save disk space; if you view that page again later, the Web browser simply re-retrieves it from the Internet.

- **Offline Web pages.** A variant of the preceding category. You can set up Internet Explorer to completely transfer some Web pages to your hard disk so you don't need to be connected to the Internet to view them. If you did this, you can delete those offline pages to save space.

- **Downloaded program files.** When you visit certain Web pages that contain programs (Java or ActiveX usually, not that it matters for your purposes here), those programs are downloaded to your PC. You can delete them.

- **Recycle Bin files.** You are probably already familiar with your PC's Recycle Bin, the place where deleted files go. You can empty this yourself from the desktop, of course, but Disk Cleanup can also do it.

To use Disk Cleanup, follow these steps:

1. Choose Start, Programs, Accessories, System Tools, Disk Cleanup. A dialog box appears from which you can select a drive.

2. Select the drive to clean up and click OK. The program analyzes the drive contents and the dialog box shown in Figure 4.8 appears.

3. Click to place or remove the check mark next to each category of files.

   To see a complete list of files in a category, select the category and click View Files. (Close the list window when finished with it.)

4. Click OK. A confirmation message appears.

5. Click Yes. Disk Cleanup removes the specified files, and the program closes.

On the More Options tab of Disk Cleanup, you'll find the following sections that point to space-saving-related parts of Windows:

⚙ **Windows Components.** Click the Clean Up button in this section to open the Windows Components tab in the Add/Remove Programs dialog box. You already know how to add and remove Windows components from Saturday Morning.

Click here to see which files fall into the selected category

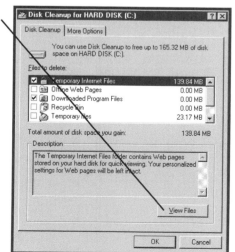

Figure 4.8

The Disk Cleanup program recommends files that can be deleted.

- ⚙ **Installed Programs.** Click the Clean Up button here to open the Install/Uninstall tab of the Add/Remove Programs dialog box. You already know from Friday Evening how to install and uninstall programs.

- ⚙ **System Restore.** Click the Clean Up button here to open the File System Properties dialog box, which contains a slider for System Restore disk space use. Drag the slider to the left to decrease the amount of space used to store System Restore files.

System Restore is a new utility in Windows Me that lets you return to earlier Windows configurations if you accidentally mess up Windows. It's covered fully in Appendix A, "Troubleshooting Problems."

Scheduling Maintenance Tasks

Some of the tools you have learned about so far in the chapter (most notably ScanDisk and Disk Defragmenter) take a long time to run and yet should be run on a regular basis. How can you remember to do so and not procrastinate running them when there are other things you would rather be doing with your PC?

One way is to use the Task Scheduler to make such programs run when you are not using your PC, so that their running does not interfere with your productivity.

Running the Maintenance Wizard

The Maintenance Wizard configures some common utilities (ScanDisk, Disk Cleanup, and Disk Defragmenter) to run automatically. You can set up using either Express or Custom modes. Express is easy and great for beginners; Custom enables you to specify when and how often each individual program should run.

To use Express scheduling, follow these steps:

1. Choose Start, Programs, Accessories, System Tools, Maintenance Wizard.

2. Choose Express, and then click Next.

3. Choose when you want the maintenance to run: Nights, Days, or Evenings. (See Figure 4.9.) Then click Next.

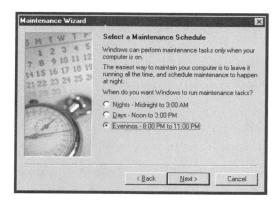

Figure 4.9

With Express setup, your only major decision is when to run the maintenance tasks.

4. (Optional) To run all the scheduled tasks for the first time right now, mark the When I click Finish, perform each scheduled task for the first time check box.

5. Click Finish.

If custom scheduling is what you want, do the following:

1. Choose Start, Programs, Accessories, System Tools, Maintenance Wizard.

2. Choose Custom, and then click Next.

3. Choose when you want the maintenance to run: Nights, Days, Evenings, or Custom. Then click Next.

4. A list appears of programs that start when Windows starts. Deselect the check box next to any of those you want to disable from starting automatically. See Figure 4.10. Then click Next.

5. To place Disk Defragmenter on the maintenance schedule, choose Yes, defragment my hard disk regularly. Then do any of the following:

   ✪ Click Reschedule to specify when it should run.

   ✪ Click Settings to change the defaults for the program.

   ✪ Click Next when you finish with the Disk Defragmenter configuration.

6. To place ScanDisk on the maintenance schedule, choose Yes, scan my hard disk for errors regularly. Then set its schedule and settings as you did for Disk Defragmenter. Click Next.

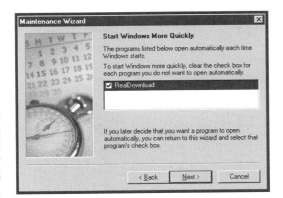

Figure 4.10

Disable any of the automatically started programs you want.

7. To place Disk Cleanup on the maintenance schedule, choose Yes, delete unnecessary files regularly. Then configure it and click Next.

8. (Optional) To run all the scheduled tasks for the first time right now, mark the When I click Finish, perform each scheduled task for the first time check box.

9. Click Finish.

Scheduling Additional Recurring Tasks

The Maintenance Wizard sets up only three specific programs, but you can use the Task Scheduler to run other programs at regular intervals too. Here's how to set one up:

1. Choose Start, Programs, Accessories, System Tools, Scheduled Tasks. The Scheduled Tasks folder appears, listing the currently scheduled tasks.

2. Double-click Add Scheduled Task. The Scheduled Task Wizard runs.

3. Click Next to begin. A list of programs installed on your PC appears, as shown in Figure 4.11.

4. Choose the program you want to schedule, and click Next.

5. Type a name for the scheduled task (or leave the default name).

6. Choose an interval at which to schedule (Daily, Weekly, and so on) and click Next.

Figure 4.11

Choose the program to schedule.

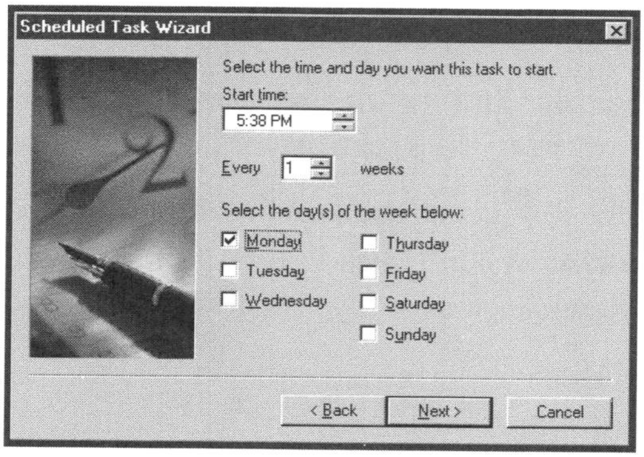

Figure 4.12

Set up the interval at which you want to schedule the program to run.

7. Set the controls that appear based on the interval you chose in step 6. For example, if you chose Weekly, you would work with the controls shown in Figure 4.12. Click Next when finished.

8. (Optional) To set advanced properties for the scheduled item, mark the Open advanced properties for this task when I click Finish check box.

Wrapping Up

This evening's session was a little shorter than the others because I know you're probably worn out after this long day of Windows study and practice! So get a good night's sleep, and tomorrow morning you'll start working with the Internet.

SUNDAY MORNING

Exploring the Internet

- ✿ A Crash Course in Internet Jargon
- ✿ Setting Up an Internet Connection
- ✿ Using Internet Explorer
- ✿ Searching on the Internet
- ✿ Sending and Receiving E-Mail with Outlook Express
- ✿ Reading Newsgroups with Outlook Express

By now I hope you're feeling comfortable with Windows itself, and are able to run programs, manage files, and set everything up just the way you like it. So, having mastered your own individual workspace, it's time to take a step outside and explore the online world of the Internet.

A Crash Course in Internet Jargon

To make sense out of this chapter, you need some basic knowledge of the Internet. If you already have some—great. See you in the next section. But if not, hold on tight and I'll take you through it very quickly.

The *Internet* is a huge network of computers all over the world. Most of the connected computers make information available to the public, and many of them provide Internet access to individuals and businesses as well.

Most ordinary people don't have computers that are directly a part of the Internet, because it's very expensive. Instead, most people get an account with an *Internet Service Provider (ISP)*, a company with a big, powerful computer that's hard-wired into the Internet full-time. You pay your monthly fee, and the service provider gives you an ID and password that let you connect to their computer and use it as an on-ramp to the Internet whenever you want to.

The most popular format for storing and retrieving information on the Internet is *Hypertext Markup Language (HTML)*. This is the format of most documents on the *World Wide Web* (or *Web* for short). While you are connected to the Internet, you can use a Web browser program that runs on your PC to request various *Web pages* from all over the world and display them on your screen. The most popular Web browser is Microsoft Internet Explorer (IE), which is built into Windows Me. A competitor is Netscape Communicator.

These Web pages are nothing more than simple text files with some HTML coding that tells the Web browser how to format the text and from what location to pull in pictures. Here is an example of some HTML coding:

```
<p>Elvis <I>lives!</I></p>
<img src="http://www.mysite.com/elvis.jpg">
```

When your Web browser receives the HTML file, it reads it as shown in Table 5.1.

TABLE 5.1   DECIPHERING SOME HTML CODING

Code	Meaning
`<p>`	Begin new paragraph
`Elvis`	Print the word "Elvis"
`<I>`	Make the text that follows italic
`lives!`	Print the word "lives!" in italic
`</I>`	Stop making text italic now
`</p>`	End the paragraph

The result shown by your Web browser looks something like this:

`Elvis ` *`lives!`*

NOTE   Don't worry—you don't have to learn any HTML coding to view pages on the Web. That's all completely behind-the-scenes.

To request a Web page from the computer that it resides on, you have to know its complete name and address; it's just like mailing a letter. This name and address is called a *Uniform Resource Locator,* or *URL* (often pronounced "earl"). A page's URL consists of http:// plus the address of the computer, a slash (/), and the name of the file itself. For example:

`http://www.acmecorp.com/~lowe/index.html`

Some HTML documents end with .htm rather than .html. Sometimes you'll see a Web address that does not have a document name, but only a site address, like this:

`http://www.acmecorp.com/~lowe`

When there is no file name, as in the previous example, most servers provide a file with the name index.html or index.htm. In other words, if I call my opening page index.html, I don't have to include its name in the address I give people when I invite them to look at my page.

You can jump from page to page with *hyperlinks*, which are *hot links* to other URLs. They're called "hot" because you can click one to make your Web browser open that URL. Hyperlinks can point to other Web pages on the same host computer, or to pages at any site anywhere in the world.

Feeling a little more comfortable with this whole Internet thing now? Good. Then move on.

Setting Up an Internet Connection

The way you set up your Internet connection depends on the type of service you have.

Most people connect using a modem, which is device that converts digital computer data to an analog signal that can pass through a phone line. Then another modem at the receiving end reverses the process. This is the type of Internet connection I focus on in this section.

Other kinds of Internet connections include network, cable modem, satellite, ISDN, and DSL. If you get one of these kinds of services, there is likely to be a technician to help you get everything set up. If you have a cable, DSL, or network Internet connection but you need help setting it up, see "Configuring a Network Connection to the Internet" later in the chapter.

Checking Your Modem's Operation

Most modems these days are plug and play—in other words, Windows detects and configures them automatically. To make sure your modem is installed and working correctly, do the following:

1. From the Control Panel, double-click Modems. The Modems Properties dialog box opens.

2. Make sure your modem is listed on the General tab.

    If it is not, click Add and work through the Add Hardware Wizard to set it up. If that doesn't work, try installing the software that came with the modem, or run through the troubleshooting help in Appendix A, "Troubleshooting Problems."

3. Click the Diagnostics tab.

4. Select the modem's COM port, as shown in Figure 5.1.

5. Click More Info.

    Windows checks the modem by sending it certain commands and noting the responses. If the modem is working correctly, results appear in a More Info box, as shown in Figure 5.2. If an error message appears instead, there is a problem with the modem.

6. Click OK, and then OK again.

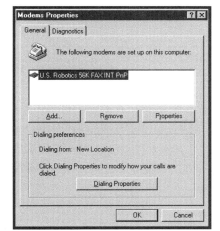

Figure 5.1

Select the modem's
port, and then click
More Info to test it.

If you run into any problems or error messages in the preceding steps, something is wrong with the modem. Perhaps it is not installed correctly, or perhaps it has a resource conflict with another device. See Appendix A for help diagnosing and fixing the problem.

OK on at least some
lines indicates that the
modem is working

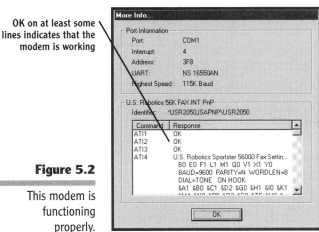

Figure 5.2

This modem is
functioning
properly.

Configuring Dial-Up Networking

Your modem communicates with your ISP's computer using the dial-up networking feature built into Windows. The easiest way to set it up is with the Internet Connection Wizard.

● ●

If you don't already have an ISP, the Internet Connection Wizard will give you a choice of several services available in your area. However, the services on the list are the ones that have paid a fee to Microsoft to be included; they are not necessarily the only or the best services available. For example, most local ISPs will not be listed. You might be able to find a better deal than the ones offered through the Internet Connection Wizard by checking with your local computer users group or watching for advertisements.

● ●

The Internet Connection Wizard (ICW) automates the process of setting up your PC for Internet connectivity. You can use it to create a new account with an ISP, or to configure your PC to use an existing account.

● ●

NOTE You can also access the Internet through an online service such as America Online (AOL). Online services provide their own software, which you set up from a CD or disk they provide, so you do not have to use the Internet Connection Wizard.

● ●

The first time you run Internet Explorer after installing Windows, the Internet Connection Wizard (ICW) runs automatically. You also might have an icon for it on your desktop. If not, you can access it by choosing Start, Programs, Accessories, Communications, Internet Connection Wizard.

The first screen of the ICW invites you to choose one of three options:

❖ *I want to sign up for a new Internet account. (My telephone line is connected to my modem.)* Choose this if you do not have an Internet account and do not know which Internet Service Provider (ISP) you want to use. The Wizard will provide several options from which you can choose.

 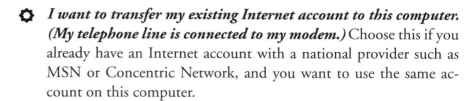
✪ *I want to transfer my existing Internet account to this computer. (My telephone line is connected to my modem.)* Choose this if you already have an Internet account with a national provider such as MSN or Concentric Network, and you want to use the same account on this computer.

✪ *I want to set up my Internet connection manually, or I want to connect through a local area network (LAN).* Choose this if you want to share an Internet connection on your LAN or if you use a local ISP that isn't likely to be on Microsoft's list of providers.

Depending on which option you choose, skip to the appropriate section that follows.

NOTE At some point during the ICW, you might see a warning that file and printer sharing is running on the same TCP/IP connection you will use to access the Internet. It lets you know that the file and printer sharing will be disabled. Click OK to continue, and then click OK to restart your computer if prompted. When you restart, the Internet Connection Wizard picks up where you left off automatically. File and printer sharing should still work even after you have disabled its association with TCP/IP; it will simply work with one of the other network protocols instead, such as IPX/SPX.

To choose a new ISP from the ones that Microsoft recommends (that is, the ones that have paid to be recommended), follow the steps in the next section. To set up an existing account in Windows, skip to the section "Setting Up an Existing Internet Account" later in the chapter.

Toward the end of the Wizard, it will ask whether you want to configure your mail account now. If you have the e-mail information (mail server names, your username, and so on), you can go ahead and do this. Or you can skip it for now, and I'll explain how to configure new e-mail accounts in Outlook Express later in this chapter.

Selected provider

Current offering

Figure 5.3

Select an offer and
click Next to
continue through
the Wizard to
sign up.

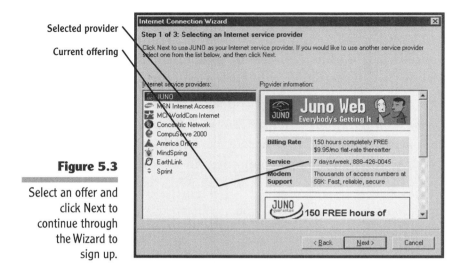

Creating a New ISP Account

If you choose to sign up for a new account from the Internet Connection
Wizard, it dials a toll-free number that retrieves a current listing of available
ISPs in your area. Review the offers for the various providers (see Figure 5.3),
select one, and then work through the Wizard to sign up for the service.

Setting Up an Existing Internet Account

Choosing the second option from the Internet Connection Wizard dials
the same toll-free number as in the preceding section and retrieves a similar
list of providers. Figure 5.4 shows the list that came up on my PC. If your
provider is listed—great. Click it. If not, choose My Internet service provider is not listed.

If your provider is one of the ones listed, select it and click Next and the
Wizard will dial your provider and help you configure the connection. The
rest of the steps in the Wizard depend on the provider.

If your provider is not listed, a message appears letting you know that you
will need to configure the connection manually. (See the following section
to learn how to do that.)

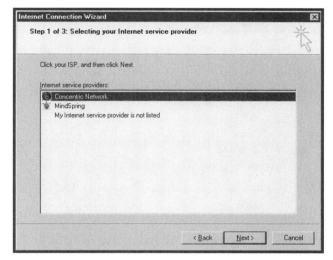

Figure 5.4

The Wizard presents a list of some of the providers in your area.

Setting Up the Internet Connection Manually

Most people end up going through the connection setup manually because at this time, the Internet Connection Wizard supports relatively few service providers directly. But don't worry—manual setup is not difficult.

To set up a new or existing account on this PC, you need the following information from your service provider:

- The telephone number for your modem to dial.

- Your username (such as `ksmith201`).

- Your password (which might be case-sensitive).

- The incoming and outgoing mail servers to use. These will probably be something like `pop.mysite.net` for the incoming and `smtp.mysite.net` for the outgoing.

- The IP address or DNS server address to use, if your provider requires that you use specific ones. These will be four sets of numbers separated by periods, such as 198.70.36.70.

Then, plug that information into the blanks provided as you work through the Wizard.

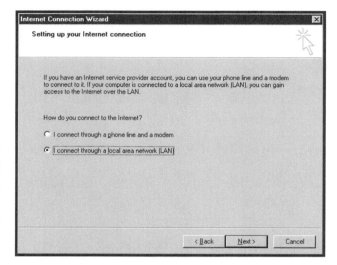

Figure 5.5

The ICW allows for the possibility that you connect through a network card rather than a modem.

Configuring a Network Connection to the Internet

If you connect to the Internet using a company network or using a cable modem or DSL connection, the connection occurs through a network card in your PC. You don't use dial-up networking because you don't have to "dial up;" the connection is always on.

To configure for networking, you can work through the ICW the same as everyone else, but when asked about how you connect to the Internet (see Figure 5.5), choose I connect through a local area network (LAN). Then just follow the prompts to complete the Wizard.

Using Internet Explorer

Internet Explorer (IE) is the Web browser that comes with Windows Me. To start it, do any of the following:

- ⚙ Click the Internet Explorer icon in the Quick Launch toolbar.
- ⚙ Double-click the Internet Explorer icon on the desktop.
- ⚙ Choose Start, Programs, Internet Explorer.

When you start IE, your home page loads. By default that's the MSN home page, but you can set it up to be any page you like. (I'll get to that later.) You can return to your home page at any time by clicking the Home button on the toolbar in Internet Explorer (the button that looks like the little house). Figure 5.6 shows the Internet Explorer window, open to the MSN home page.

Figure 5.6, like most Web pages, has two types of hyperlinks: text and graphical. The mouse pointer in Figure 5.6 is pointing at a text hyperlink, which looks like underlined text. A graphical hyperlink is a picture with a hyperlink associated with it. When you click the picture, or the underlined text, a different Web page loads or the display jumps to a different part of the same page.

As you move forward from the home page, the Back button becomes available. You can click it to return to the previously viewed page. If you do so, the Forward button then becomes available and takes you back where you were. The Home button returns you to your home page at any time.

Back button

Forward button

Stop button

Refresh button

Home button

Mouse pointer becomes a hand when over a hyperlink

Figure 5.6

Internet Explorer, open to the MSN home page that's the default when you install Windows Me.

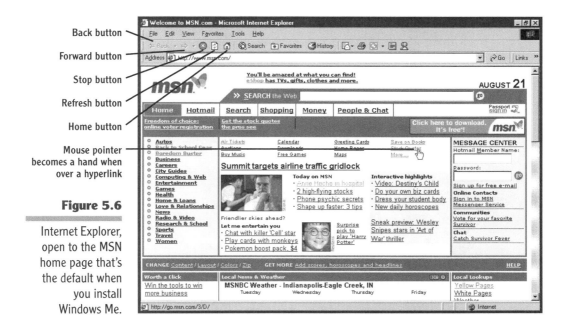

TIP

■■

The Forward and Back buttons have down arrows on them; clicking the down arrow opens a drop-down list of pages from which you can choose. For example, you can open the Back button's list and select the fourth page down on the list to go back four pages at once, rather than clicking the Back button four times.

■■

The Stop button, labeled in Figure 5.6, stops a page from loading. (It's active only when a page is loading.) If a page seems to be taking forever to load, sometimes I'll use Stop to abort it. The Refresh button reloads the same page that is currently displayed.

Surfing the Web with Hyperlinks

Browsing Web content is called "surfing" because you jump from one page to another by clicking hyperlinks. For example, you might start out reading an article about a pop star, and then click a link to see a picture of that star at a photo gallery site, and then jump to a site that sells digital cameras for creating your own online pictures, and then jump to a site of a credit card company offering you a credit card with which to make online purchases. You get the idea. Surfing the Web is like free-association thought, with one idea leading to a tangential one. To surf, simply click a hyperlink.

Going to a Specific Web Page

One way of getting to a Web page is to directly enter its URL in the Address box in IE. To do so, just type the address and press Enter or click the Go button. For example, Figure 5.7 shows the result of entering http://www.primapub.com.

Managing Your Favorites List

Open the Favorites menu in IE, and you'll see several shortcuts to various Web sites you can visit, neatly categorized. Most of these sites are either owned by Microsoft or paying Microsoft a fee to be there, so their "Best of the Web" category is not exactly objective. Still, there is some quality content to peruse here. To go to one of the pages, simply select it from the Favorites menu.

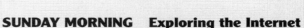

Type the address here

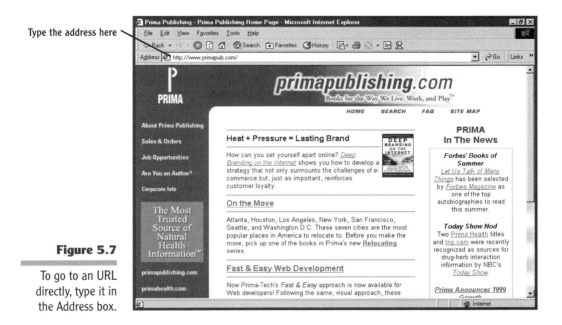

Figure 5.7

To go to an URL directly, type it in the Address box.

You can also open the Favorites menu in a separate pane, to the left of the main one. To do so, click the Favorites button on the toolbar. When you do so, the Favorites list in the new pane becomes a list of hyperlinks you can click to visit the various pages. You can click a folder to see the list of Web pages within it. For example, Figure 5.8 shows the Media folder (which is also the Media submenu on the Favorites menu). To close that pane, click the X in its top-right corner, or simply click the Favorites button on the toolbar again to toggle it off.

Adding an URL to the Favorites List

As you just saw, the Favorites list comes with some interesting pages to visit, but you will probably want to add your own favorites to it as well. Even if you've only been using the Web for the last 15 minutes, you have probably already found a Web page that you want to be able to refer to again later. By adding it to your Favorites list, you create an easy-to-access shortcut to it.

Favorites pane

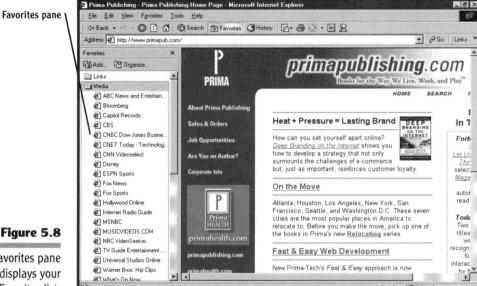

Figure 5.8

The Favorites pane displays your Favorites list.

To add an URL to your Favorites list:

1. Display the page in IE.

2. Choose Favorites, Add to Favorites.

3. In the Add Favorite dialog box, confirm the name of the page, or type a different name if desired. This is the text that will appear on the menu for that URL.

4. If you want to place the item in a submenu, click the Create in button, and then click the folder where you want to store it. See Figure 5.9.

    You don't have to choose a submenu for the item; you can add it directly to the Favorites menu. You can also create a new folder if desired by clicking the New Folder button.

5. Click OK.

These are some folders I have already created for organizing my favorites.

Figure 5.9

Confirm how you want the page's name to appear on the list, and select a folder for it on the Favorites menu.

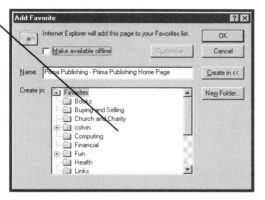

Removing URLs from Your Favorites List

You can remove items from your Favorites list as easily as you added them. (More easily, even!) One way is to open the Favorites menu, and then right-click the item and choose Delete from its shortcut menu. Here's another way:

1. Choose Favorites, Organize Favorites.

2. Select the item to delete.

3. Click the Delete button.

4. Click Close.

You can also use either of the previous procedures to delete entire folders.

Rearranging or Restructuring the Favorites List

Besides adding and removing favorites, you can also move them around. You can change the order in which the items and folders appear on the Favorites menu by simply dragging them up or down on the list in the Organize Favorites dialog box. You can also move an item to a different folder.

Choose Favorites, Organize Favorites, and then:

○ To rename a favorite, select it and click Rename. Type a new name and click OK.

⚙ To create a new folder, click Create Folder. Type a name and press Enter.

⚙ To move an item up or down on the list, click and drag it.

⚙ To move an item to a different folder, select it and click Move to Folder. A Browse for Folder box appears; click where you want to move it, and then click OK.

Working with the History List

The History list is like the Favorites list except it's a complete history of everywhere you've been on the Web recently. To use the History list, click the History button on the toolbar. The History list then opens in a separate pane, as shown in Figure 5.10. This is great in case you forget to save a particular Web site to your Favorites list but want to go back there later anyway.

History list

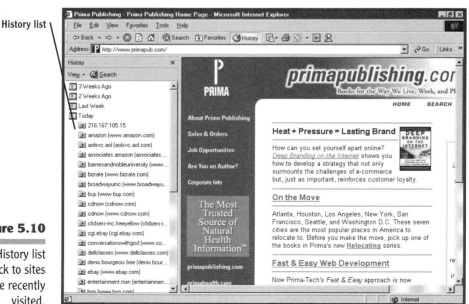

Figure 5.10

Use the History list to go back to sites you've recently visited.

TIP As you can see, the History list automatically shows all your guilty secrets of where you've been online. To clear the History list and thereby erase your tracks, choose Tools, Internet Options and click the Clear History button.

Using Web Content

What can you do with Web content, besides reading it onscreen? Well, you can save a Web page in a file on your hard disk, or print a page, or e-mail a page to a friend (or to yourself even!).

Printing in Internet Explorer

To print a single copy of the current Web page, click the Print button on the toolbar in IE.

If you want to set some print options, such as choosing the page range, the number of copies, or the printer to use, choose File, Print instead. This opens the Print dialog box.

The Print dialog box is much like that of any other program you work with, except for the Frames setting. This is active only when you are printing a Web page that has multiple frames (that is, multiple panes), and it specifies how you want a multi-frame page to print:

- The As laid out onscreen option prints the page just as it appears.

- The Only the selected frame option prints only the contents of the frame you last clicked in before issuing the Print command.

- The All frames option individually prints each frame on a separate page.

If the page you are printing doesn't have multiple frames, the previous options will be unavailable, as in Figure 5.11.

Saving a Web Page to Your Hard Disk

When you view a Web page, your browser does not save that whole page to your hard disk; it just displays it. When you disconnect from the Internet, that page will no longer be available for viewing until you log back on again.

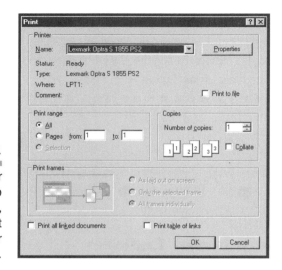

Figure 5.11

Internet Explorer lets you print Web pages that you find, much like you print in a word processor or other program.

An exception to a Web page not being saved to your hard disk is if the page is saved in your browser's cache. The *cache*, a.k.a. temporary Internet files, is a storage repository of pages you have visited; your Web browser stores copies of them in case you want to go back to a certain page, to help it reload that page faster. When the cache gets full, the oldest items in it drop out. Like the History list, the cache can show a snooper where you've been. To clear the cache, choose Tools, Internet Options and click Delete Files in the Temporary Internet Files section of the dialog box.

Use the File, Save As command in IE to save the currently displayed Web page to your hard disk, so you can refer back to it later when you are not online.

When you save a Web page, you choose what format you want to save it in:

○ The Web Page, complete option saves the entire page, including any helper files it needs to display correctly, such as graphics or style sheets.

○ The Web Archive for e-mail option saves all the information needed to display the page in a single MIME-encoded file, with no separate helper files. This is suitable for e-mailing.

⚙ The Web Page, HTML only option saves only the current Web page's HTML text, not the graphics or other helper files.

⚙ Text File. Saves only the text from the current Web page, in a plain unformatted state.

Web Page, complete is the default, and is usually your best choice. If the page contains a lot of graphics that you aren't interested in saving, Web Page, HTML only might be a better choice. Its saves your hard disk space by not saving anything except the text and the HTML formatting codes.

E-Mailing a Web Page

To e-mail a Web page, choose File, Send, Page by E-mail. This encodes the current Web page in an e-mail body and opens your e-mail program so you can specify a recipient. (More about the Outlook Express e-mail program later in the chapter.) If your e-mail program does not support HTML within a message body, it will place the Web page in an attachment instead of in the body.

If you choose File, Send, Page as Attachment, it starts a new e-mail in your default e-mail program and includes the currently displayed Web page as a file attachment.

NOTE It is more efficient to send someone the address of a Web page in an e-mail than to mail them the whole page. However, if the page is time-sensitive, such as a story on a news site, you might want to mail the whole page in case it's gone by the time your recipient reads your note.

Saving a Graphic from a Web Page

To copy a graphic from a Web page to your hard disk, right-click it and choose Save Picture As. Choose a location, change the file name if desired, and click Save. See Figure 5.12.

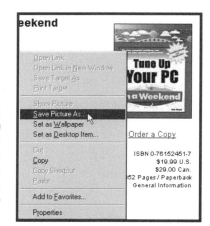

Figure 5.12

Right-click a
graphic and
complete the Save
As dialog box to
copy it to your
own PC.

CAUTION In many cases, the pictures on a Web site are copyrighted, and it is illegal to take them without consent. Be sure to check this out before you download a graphic.

Searching on the Internet

There is no one comprehensive directory of the Internet, but there are several good ones. In most cases, you go to a particular search Web site, enter the words you are looking for, and press Enter. A list of Web pages appears that matches your criteria.

Internet Explorer has a built-in Search facility that draws upon several of the most popular search sites. To use it, click the Search button on the toolbar. A Search pane appears to the left of the main window. Enter what you are searching for and click OK, and you're on your way. See Figure 5.13. To close the Search pane, click its Close button or click the Search button on the toolbar again.

Here are some other search sites you might find useful, in no particular order. All are good, reputable sites with tons of Web pages in their listings:

- ✪ **AltaVista.** http://www.altavista.com
- ✪ **Webcrawler.** http://www.webcrawler.com

Here's what I entered

These Web pages matched my keywords

I clicked a hyperlink to display this page

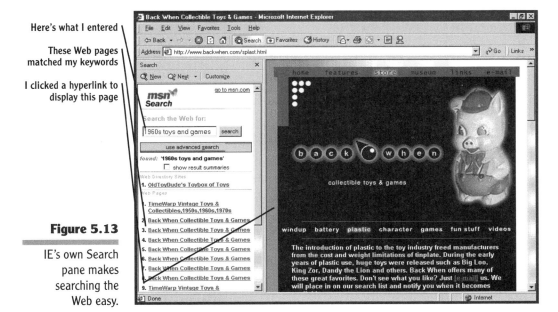

Figure 5.13

IE's own Search pane makes searching the Web easy.

⚙ **Yahoo!.** http://www.yahoo.com

⚙ **Metacrawler.** http://www.metacrawler.com

⚙ **Ask Jeeves.** http://www.askjeeves.com

⚙ **Excite.** http:/www.excite.com

⚙ **MSN.** http://www.msnsearch.com

TIP If a Web address starts with www., you can omit the http:// part when typing it in; IE will know what you want.

Protecting Yourself and Your Family Online

You've probably heard about all the dangers of the Internet, from credit card theft to child pornography. Those dangers do exist, but they're not nearly as pressing and prevalent as some people might want you to believe.

In the following sections, I tell you about Internet Explorer's security features and content filter, which can give the worried Web surfer some peace of mind.

Security Settings in IE

IE's security features ask you to trade off functionality for security. You need to decide how secure you want to be and balance that with how many of the newest Web features you want to take advantage of. The highest security levels let you surf completely anonymously, but those settings also prevent you from participating in things like online ordering, multimedia content, and Internet games.

So what is it exactly that people are afraid of, and securing against? There are two main threats: 1) malicious program code on Web pages running and doing bad things to your PC, and 2) privacy invasion, where a Web site owner collects information about you or your PC without your consent.

Security is divided into four zones: Internet, Local Intranet, Trusted Sites, and Restricted Sites. Internet is a catch-all zone into which everything falls that is not a part of one of the other three zones. The other three zones allow you to add and remove sites from their list (with the Sites button). So, for example, if there's a particular site with a game that you like to play, you can add it to your Trusted Sites list, and then set the security level for trusted sites to Medium-Low so the game will work. You can then leave your Internet zone set to Medium or High.

Your security level choices are: High (very secure but can't do much), Medium (fairly secure), Medium-Low (the lowest recommended setting except for Intranet or Trusted Sites), and Low (no security at all to speak of). You can also define custom security levels for each zone.

To view and change the security settings in IE, do the following:

1. Choose Tools, Internet Options.

2. Click the Security tab.

3. Click the icon for the zone you want to set a security rating for.

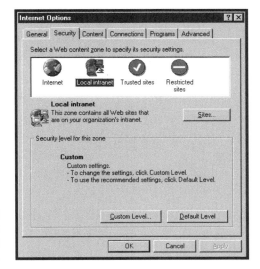

Figure 5.14

Set a security rating
for each zone.

4. Choose a security level by dragging the slider up or down.

   Or, if you prefer, click the Custom Level button and set individual security properties for the zone. See Figure 5.14.

NOTE When you click Custom Level, you see a long list of check boxes for individual security features to turn on/off. Custom Level won't make much sense to the average user, but can come in handy if you are directed by a certain Web site to change a particular security setting in order to use the content there. For example, some Web sites need for you to enable certain Java-based security settings.

5. Repeat steps 3 and 4 for each zone.

6. Click OK.

Content Filters

If you have underage children who use your PC, you might be concerned about your children being exposed to X-rated content online, or excessive violence or bigotry. IE provides a simple content rating feature that can help prevent some of the more obvious nastiness from reaching your desktop. However, it is not perfect and can't be relied on 100%. There are other add-on programs you can buy that do a more thorough job.

The Content Advisor in IE compares the settings you choose to the ratings for a particular site. Not all sites have ratings, so you need to decide whether you want sites that have no rating to be viewable. You can also choose a password that can be typed to override a block on a site.

To set up content restrictions:

1. Choose Tools, Internet Options.

2. Click the Content tab, and then click the Enable button. The Content Advisor opens.

3. Select a category from the list (Language, Nudity, Sex, or Violence).

4. Drag the slider bar to choose an acceptable level for that category. For example, in Figure 5.15, the Nudity rating is set to Level 3.

5. Repeat steps 3 and 4 for each category.

6. (Optional) To block or allow certain sites, click the Approved Sites tab, type the address of a site, and then click Always to always allow it or Never to always block it. Repeat for other sites as desired.

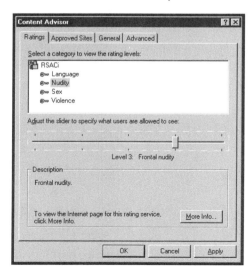

Figure 5.15

Set the rating for each category.

7. Click the General tab, and then select or deselect the Users can see sites that have no rating check box. When this is marked, all unrated sites are assumed to be objectionable.

8. (Optional) To set a password to override the block, select the Supervisor can type a password to allow users to view restricted content check box. Then click Change Password to set the password.

9. (Optional) To find and use other rating systems, click the Find Rating Systems button. This takes you to a Web page with the latest information.

10. When you're done, click OK. A Create Supervisor Password box appears.

11. Enter a password, and then type it again to confirm. Then click OK. This prevents others from turning off the rating system.

12. A confirmation message appears; click OK.

13. Click OK to close the Internet Options dialog box.

When someone visits a site that violates the ratings set, a message will appear, as in Figure 5.16. You can then type in the supervisor password, or click Cancel.

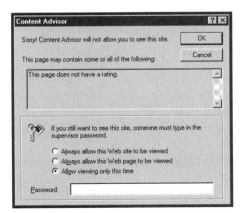

Figure 5.16

This message appears when a content rating prevents a page from being displayed.

Firewalls

With a dial-up Internet connection employing a modem, each time you connect your provider assigns you a different IP address (a numeric identifier—let's just leave it at that, without getting too techie). Because it changes each time you connect, the chances of someone hacking into your computer using that number are slim.

However, with a high-speed Internet connection such as cable or DSL, you're connected all the time and you have a static IP address—that is, the same address all the time. The longer an IP address exists online, the more likely it is to be hacked. "Hacked" means that some computer techie person is able to gain access to your PC and snoop around, possibly changing or deleting files or infecting it with a virus. That's why many people with static IP addresses want some extra protection.

One way to protect yourself is to disable file and printer sharing on the PC. (You do this through the Network icon in the Control Panel; there's a File and Printer Sharing button in that dialog box.) Another is to use a firewall.

A firewall is hardware or software that prevents anything from coming into your PC through the Internet that you don't specifically authorize. There are various types of firewalls. The professional-quality ones are usually a separate piece of hardware that your Internet cable passes through on the way to your PC. However, home users can achieve much the same result with software such as Norton Internet Security, BlackIce, or ZoneAlarm.

Personally, I have had good luck using ZoneAlarm. Plus, it's free to individuals, and you can download it from the Internet at http://www.zonealarm.com. This program runs in your system tray all the time, and lets you specify which programs and computers can access your computer, both incoming and outgoing. Figure 5.17 shows the ZoneAlarm Control Panel. Its settings are like those in Internet Explorer but much more complex.

Take a Break

Now that you're a Web surfing master, take a few minutes of time-out to enjoy that fact. Explore the Web. Search for your favorite subjects. Look

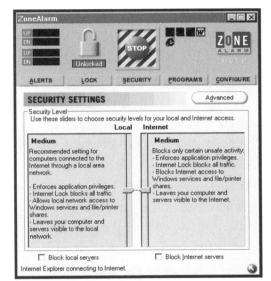

Figure 5.17

ZoneAlarm is an easy-to-use firewall program that's free for home users.

up long-lost relatives. Then continue to the next section, where you'll learn about electronic mail, or e-mail.

Sending and Receiving E-Mail with Outlook Express

There are a lot of different e-mail systems out there. They can roughly be broken down into three categories:

- **POP-based e-mail.** These are the most powerful and flexible. They require an e-mail program such as Outlook or Outlook Express. If you have an Internet account with an ISP, you probably have at least one POP e-mail account.

- **Web-based e-mail.** This is e-mail that you can read and write from a Web site. Examples include Yahoo! mail, Hotmail, and so on. These mail accounts are usually free, and have nothing to do with your ISP.

- **Outlook Express.** Outlook Express can be used with these, but unless yours is Hotmail you will need to know the exact name of the mail sever, which can be tricky to determine. You are also free to continue reading and writing from the Web, and forget about using Outlook Express.

⚙ **Online Service e-mail.** If you use America Online or some other online service to connect to the Internet, you probably have an e-mail address and an Inbox on that service. You use the online service software to manage it. You cannot use Outlook Express with this kind of e-mail.

In this chapter, I'll assume that a) you have an e-mail account that can be used with Outlook Express, and b) you want to use Outlook Express as your e-mail software. Outlook Express comes free with Windows Me. If that's not the case, feel free to skip this section on Outlook Express.

If you have Microsoft Office, you also have Outlook, a program that not only manages e-mail but also keeps track of addresses, to-do lists, and calendar items. You're free to use Outlook if you want, but you cannot follow the steps in this chapter word-for-word.

Starting Outlook Express

To start Outlook Express, you can do any of the following:

⚙ Click the Outlook Express icon in the Quick Launch toolbar.

⚙ Double-click the Outlook Express icon on the desktop.

⚙ Choose Start, Programs, Outlook Express.

When Outlook Express opens, its Start page appears, shown in Figure 5.18. To go to your e-mail inbox, click Inbox in the folder tree to the left, or click the Read Mail hyperlink.

If you want to go directly to the inbox in the future, mark the When Outlook Express starts, go directly to my inbox check box.

Setting Up a Mail Account

If you have not yet set up a mail account, the Internet Connection Wizard will prompt you to do so the first time you start Outlook Express. Follow

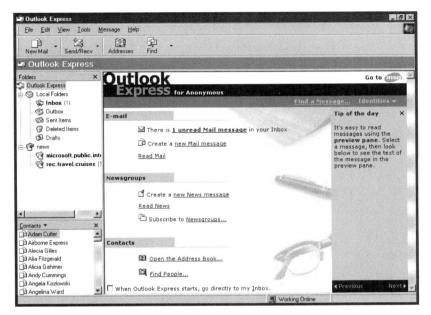

Figure 5.18

The Outlook Express Start screen

the prompts, filling in the information provided to you by your ISP, to get the job done. You'll need the following information:

- E-mail address.

- The name you want to appear as your name in people's inboxes (it need not match your e-mail address).

- Your incoming mail server. This is probably "pop." or "mail." followed by whatever comes after the @ in your e-mail address, like this: pop.mysite.com.

- Your outgoing mail server. This is probably "smtp." or "mail." followed by whatever comes after the @ in your e-mail address.

If you have already configured your mail account but want to add another e-mail account to Outlook Express, you are free to do so. For example, perhaps you have several POP e-mail addresses and you want to get your mail from all of them in one place. This can be the case, for example, if you have a Web site that you host with a different company from the one you use as your ISP.

To set up another e-mail account:

1. Choose Tools, Accounts.

2. Click the Add button, and then select Mail. The Internet Connection Wizard runs.

3. Enter the name by which you want to be known, and then click Next.

4. Enter the e-mail address you want to set up. Then click Next.

5. Open the Incoming Mail Server drop-down list and choose the type of mail server. If it's a Web-based e-mail account, choose HTTP. If it's a POP mail account, choose POP3. The third type, IMAP, is rather specialized; you probably don't have that type.

6. If you chose POP3 or IMAP, enter the incoming and outgoing mail servers in the boxes provided. See Figure 5.19. Then click Next.

7. Enter your e-mail address and mail password in the boxes provided; then click Next.

8. Click Finish. Your mail account is now set up and you're ready to start sending and receiving mail!

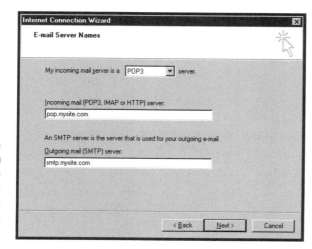

Figure 5.19

Tell Outlook Express about the mail server from which you want to get your mail.

The regular Inbox

The Hotmail Inbox

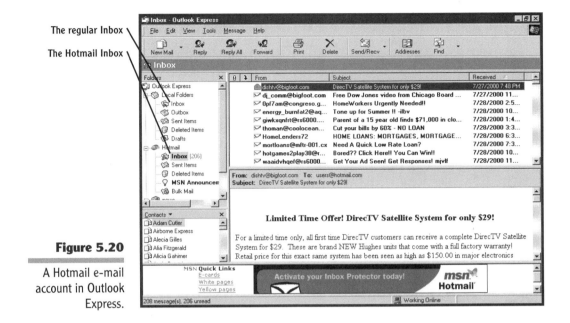

Figure 5.20

A Hotmail e-mail
account in Outlook
Express.

If you added an HTML mail server, you'll see a message asking whether
you want to download folders from the mail server you added; click Yes to
do so. Your Hotmail (or other HTML) mail will appear in a different inbox,
and a different part of the folder tree in Outlook Express, than your regular
POP mail. See Figure 5.20 for an example.

Receiving E-Mail

When you start Outlook Express, it automatically connects to your mail
server(s) and retrieves your new e-mail. You can also ask it to send and
receive at any time by doing any of the following:

- Clicking the Send/Recv button on the toolbar

- Pressing Ctrl+M

- Choosing Tools, Send and Receive, Send and Receive All

If you have multiple e-mail accounts, each one can be included in a default send/receive operation or not. To do so:

1. Choose Tools, Accounts.

2. On the Mail tab, double-click the mail server.

3. On the General tab, select or deselect the Include this account when receiving mail or synchronizing check box.

4. Click OK.

To send and receive for a specific account only, choose Tools, Send and Receive and then select that particular account.

Your incoming mail appears in your Inbox. POP mail appears in the Inbox under Local Folders, whereas Hotmail appears in the Inbox under Hotmail.

Reading E-Mail

Your Inbox is divided into four panes. The top-left pane lists the available folders, just like in Windows Explorer. The bottom-left pane lists e-mail addresses you have saved in your Address book. The top-right pane lists the e-mail messages in your Inbox, and the bottom-right pane previews the selected e-mail. See Figure 5.21.

You can read an e-mail by selecting it and then scrolling through the preview pane, or by double-clicking the message to open it in a separate window. New messages appear in bold, so you can distinguish them from those you've already read.

Figure 5.22 shows a message in its own window. Notice that the toolbar buttons change to those appropriate for dealing with that message, rather than general-purpose Outlook Express buttons. This message has lots of cool formatting; you'll learn about formatting the messages you send later in the chapter.

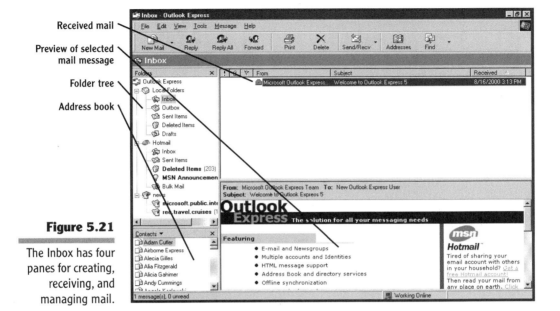

Received mail

Preview of selected mail message

Folder tree

Address book

Figure 5.21

The Inbox has four panes for creating, receiving, and managing mail.

Toolbar buttons for handling the message

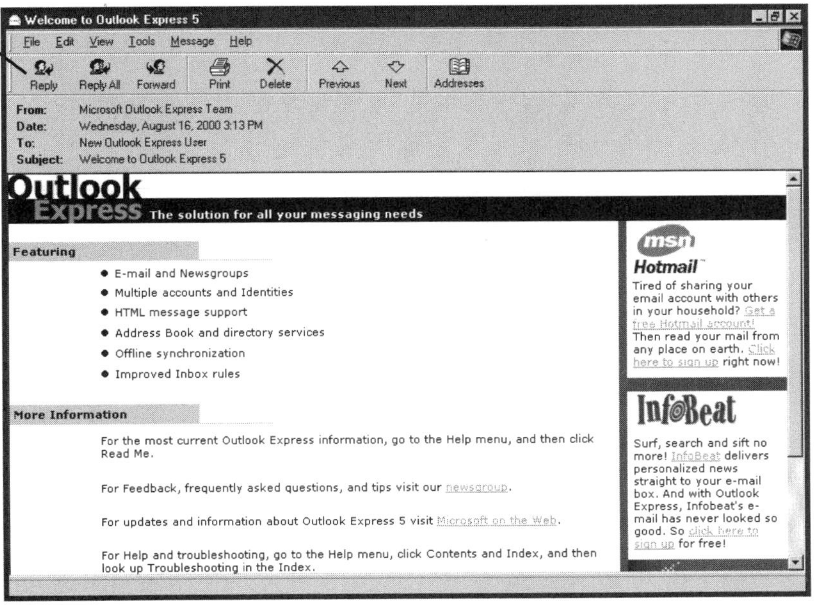

Figure 5.22

A received message in its own window

Printing a Message

To print a message, either display it by double-clicking it or simply choose it from the Inbox. Then click the Print button or choose File, Print.

Reading and Saving an Attachment

Some messages you receive have attachments—that is, other files sent along with the message. An attachment can be a forwarded message, a picture, a compressed archive, a document, or any other file type. If a message has an attachment, a paper clip icon appears next to it in the Inbox. When you open the message in its own pane, the attachment appears on the Attach line. See Figure 5.23.

To save an e-mail attachment to your hard disk, do the following:

1. Select the message in the Inbox, or double-click it to open it in its own window.

2. Choose File, Save Attachments. The Save Attachments dialog box opens.

3. Click Browse and choose the folder and drive in which to save the attachment.

4. Click Save. The attached file is saved there.

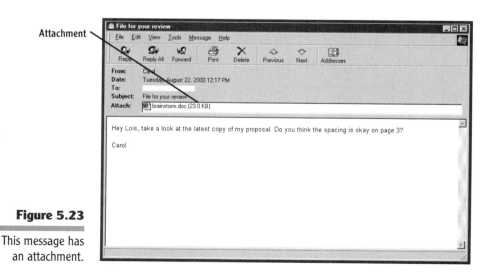

Figure 5.23

This message has an attachment.

Figure 5.24

You can open an attachment from the Preview pane by clicking the paper clip.

You do not have to save an attachment to view it. Just do any of the following to open the attachment in whatever program its extension is associated with:

✿ When the message is open in its own window, double-click the attachment name on the Attach line.

✿ In the message preview pane under the inbox, click the large paper clip in the top-right corner. A menu opens showing the attachments. Click the attachment to open it. See Figure 5.24.

Deleting an E-Mail

To delete a message, select it on the Inbox listing and press Delete or click the Delete button on the toolbar. This moves the message to the Deleted Items folder, just like deleting a file in Windows moves it to the Recycle Bin.

If you change your mind, you can undelete a message by viewing the Deleted Items folder and dragging the message back onto the Inbox icon in the folder tree.

Just as you can empty the Recycle Bin in Windows, you can clear the Deleted Items folder. Just switch to that folder, select the messages to delete, and press the Delete key.

Replying to E-Mail

You can reply to any message you receive simply by clicking the Reply button on the toolbar and typing your response. When you reply, the original message appears quoted in the message pane. Each line of it is preceded by a symbol (the default is a solid bar) that indicates the text is quoted and not original. You can type your reply above the quoted block, or you can insert the lines of your reply between the quoted lines to respond individually to certain points that the writer made. Figure 5.25 shows an example.

To reply to a received message:

1. Select the message.

2. Click the Reply button.

3. Type your reply.

4. Click Send.

When you click Send, the message moves to the Outbox folder. It will be sent the next time Outlook Express sends and receives. To send immediately, click the Send/Recv button.

When you reply to a message, its icon in the inbox changes to an envelope with a left-pointing arrow in its corner. (In contrast, when you forward a message, covered later in the chapter, the icon changes to an envelope with a *right*-pointing arrow.)

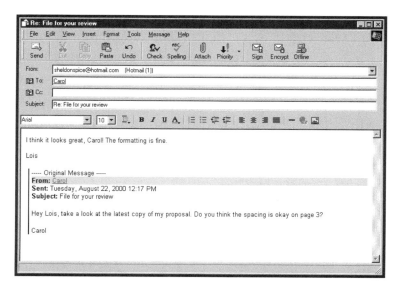

Figure 5.25

Replying to a message

Composing New E-Mail

Composing a new message is just like replying except you specify a recipient and a subject. You can look up the recipient in your address book, or type the address manually.

There are several ways of starting a new message:

- Double-click a name in your Address Book pane to start a new message and address it to that person.

- Choose File, New, Mail Message.

- Click the New Message button on the toolbar.

- Click the Addresses button, and then select a person's name and click the Action button. Select Send Mail on the menu that opens.

Any way you do it, a new message window opens. From there, just fill in the recipient's e-mail address (if it's not there already), the subject, and your message text. See Figure 5.26.

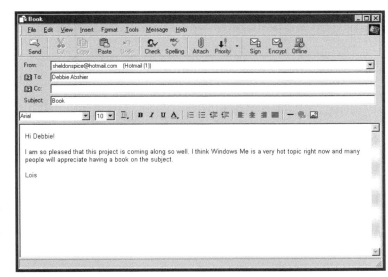

Figure 5.26

A new message, composed and ready to send by clicking the Send button

NOTE If you have more than one e-mail account set up in Outlook Express, you can choose which account to use by opening the From box's drop-down list and choosing a different mail account.

If you are typing the addresses of more than one recipient, separate the address with semicolons.

You can look up recipients in your address book by clicking the To button. This opens your address book, shown in Figure 5.27. Click a name, and then click the To button to move it to the To list. The CC and BCC fields are for FYI copies for other people. CC is a regular copy, with the name appearing on the sent message. BCC is a blind copy, where the BCC recipient's name is hidden. Click OK to return to composing the message.

When the message is ready, click the Send button to send it, just as you did with the reply in the previous section.

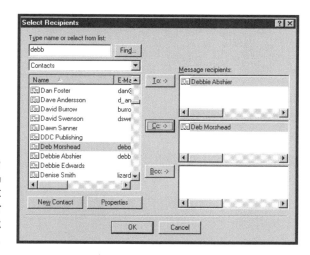

Figure 5.27

You can insert recipients from your address book if desired.

Forwarding E-Mail

Forwarding mail is just like replying to it, except instead of the message going back to the original writer, it goes "forward" to someone else. To forward a message:

1. Select the message.

2. Click the Forward button on the toolbar.

3. Type or choose a recipient.

4. Type any comments you want to make at the top of the message.

5. Click Send.

Working with the Address Book

You can add someone to the address book in several ways. One of the easiest ways is to copy the address from a message you've received. The person need not have been the sender; he or she can be one of the other recipients. Here's how to do it:

1. Double-click the message to display it in its own window.

2. Choose Tools, Add to Address Book, and then choose Sender to add the sender or choose one of the other addresses to add it instead. A Properties box appears for that person.

3. (Optional) To file the person under his or her real name (not the e-mail address), click the Name tab and type the correct first, middle, and last names into the boxes provided.

4. Click OK.

You can also add new addresses directly to the address book. To do so:

1. From the Inbox, click the Addresses button on the toolbar.

2. Click the New button, and choose New Contact. A new Properties box appears for a new person.

3. Type the person's e-mail address in the E-mail Addresses box, and click Add.

4. Enter the person's first, middle, and last name if desired. (You can omit any or all of those fields to list the person by e-mail address only.)

5. Click OK, adding the person to the address book.

6. Close the Address Book window.

Adding an Attachment

You can send pictures, documents, and other files to your friends and family through the Attachment feature of Outlook Express. To attach a file to a message, just click the Attach button on the toolbar as you are composing it. You can attach files to new messages, to replies, or to forwards.

1. Click the Attach button. The Insert Attachment dialog box opens.

2. Select the file to attach. To select more than one file, hold down Ctrl as you click each one.

3. Click Attach.

4. Finish and send the e-mail normally.

◆ ◆

CAUTION Large attachment files take a long time to send and receive. If the recipient has a slow e-mail connection, it might take a long time for your message to download to his or her PC. Some ISPs even put a size limit on incoming e-mail, and reject any e-mail with an attachment larger than a specified size. Check with the person to whom you are sending beforehand to make sure a large attachment is welcome.

◆ ◆

Formatting Your Message

You can send messages in Plan Text or Rich Text Format (RTF). Rich Text lets you apply formatting such as bold, italic, underlining, colors, and so on.

Not everyone's e-mail programs can accept messages in RTF, so if you aren't sure, it's best to send your message in Plain Text. However, if you are sure the recipient can accept RTF messages, you might want to experiment with Outlook Express's formatting tools.

To format a message:

1. If the formatting toolbar in your message composition window is unavailable, choose Format, Rich Text (HTML).

2. Use the Formatting toolbar in the mail composition window to format the message, just as you do in a word processing program such as Word.

   For example, you can add bullets and horizontal lines, change the font and text size, add pictures, and so on. Figure 5.28 shows a message with various types of formatting applied.

3. If desired, choose Format, Background, Color and select a background color for the message.

4. Complete and send the message normally.

Horizontal line

Colored background

Different font and size

Bold, italic, and underlined

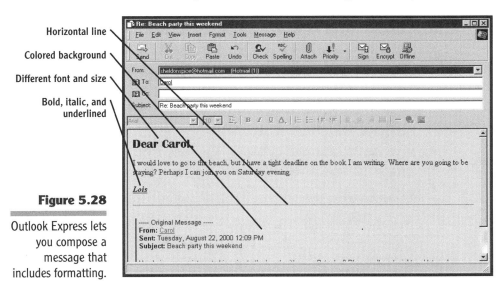

Figure 5.28

Outlook Express lets you compose a message that includes formatting.

TIP If you are sending a message to someone with Outlook or Outlook Express as their mail program, you might want to play around with the Stationery feature in Outlook Express. It uses a graphic as a background to the message to make it look like you are typing on fancy stationery. To choose a stationery design, choose Format, Apply Stationery.

Reading Newsgroups with Outlook Express

Newsgroups are like public bulletin boards where anybody can post a message. One person leaves a message; someone else posts a reply (again, which everyone can read); and so on. It's like e-mail en masse. You'll be amazed at the number and variety of newsgroups (over 35,000 at last count), and the zeal with which some people participate in them!

Outlook Express has a Newsreader feature that you can use to read and post to newsgroups, and that's what you'll learn about in this final section of this evening's session.

Setting Up a News Account

Your ISP likely provides a news server as well as a mail server, and its name is probably "news." plus whatever comes after the @ sign in your e-mail address, like this: news.myisp.com. A *news server* is a computer that stores messages from a variety of newsgroups and provides those messages on-demand to any users who request them through a news reader program such as Outlook Express.

If your news server is already set up in Outlook Express, it will appear at the bottom of the folder tree. But if not, do the following to set it up.

1. In Outlook Express, choose Tools, Accounts.

2. Click the News tab. Then click Add, and then News. The Internet Connection Wizard appears.

3. Type the name by which you want to be known in the newsgroup postings in the Display Name box, and then click Next. You might not want to use your real name for privacy reasons.

4. Enter your e-mail address in the Email address box, and then click Next.

5. Type the news server address in the News (NNTP) Server box.

NOTE Some services that use static IP addresses, such as cable modems, will let you enter simply "news" in the News Server box; you don't have to enter the full name of the server.

6. If the news server requires a login (most do not), mark the My news server requires me to log on check box. Then click Next.

7. If you marked the check box in step 6, a prompt appears for your username and password. Enter them and click Next. Skip to step 8 if this doesn't apply to you.

8. Click Finish. The new account appears on the account list.

9. Click Close to close the Internet Accounts dialog box.

10. You're asked whether you want to retrieve a list of newsgroups from the server; click Yes and wait for the list to appear.

11. Subscribe to the newsgroups you want, as explained in the following section.

You should have to set up your news server only once unless you want to use a different news server at some point.

NOTE Besides your ISP's news server, you might be able to connect to other news severs as well, such as one provided by a software manufacturer for discussion of their products. Get the signup information from the individual companies, usually from their Web sites.

Subscribing to a Newsgroup

Each ISP or news server service decides which newsgroups it will carry on its server. More than 35,000 are available, but some of them (okay, a lot of them) are just pornography links, so some providers choose to exclude

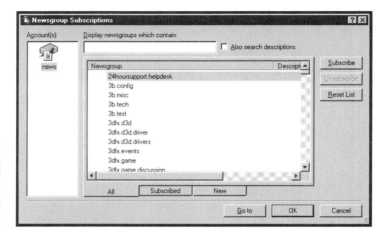

Figure 5.29

The list of
newsgroups carried
by your news server
appears here.

some of the more graphic ones. If your provider doesn't carry a particular newsgroup you want, you can always request it.

The list of newsgroups might already be onscreen at this point if you just finished setting up your news account. If not, click the news server's name on the folder tree, and then click the Newsgroups button on the toolbar to open the list. See Figure 5.29.

You can scroll through the list to locate groups that interest you, and then click the Subscribe button when you find one you want.

You can narrow down the list by typing a certain word in the Display newsgroups which contain box. For example, to narrow down the list to only groups having to do with vacations, type **Vacation**.

When you are done subscribing to groups, click OK. Now the groups you chose appear beneath the news server name on the folder tree, and you can view a group's messages by selecting it from there.

To unsubscribe to a group, right-click it on the folder tree and choose Unsubscribe.

Reading Newsgroup Messages

After you subscribe to the groups you want, they appear in the folder tree. Just click the group you want to read, and its messages appear, much like messages in your e-mail inbox. See Figure 5.30.

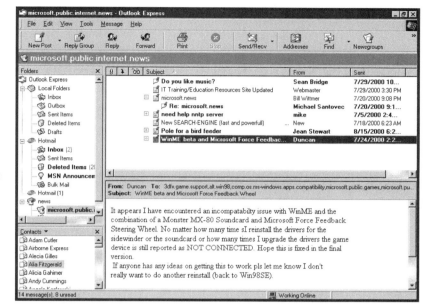

Figure 5.30

The messages from the selected newsgroup appear. Bold indicates unread messages. A plus sign means there are replies to be displayed.

To read a message, click it to make it appear in the preview pane, or double-click it to open it in a separate window, just like with e-mail.

Some messages have plus signs next to them; click the plus sign to expand the list of replies to that message.

TIP

You can sort messages according to any of the columns by clicking the column name. Click it again to change between ascending and descending order. You can also resize columns by dragging the divider between the column headings.

When you read a message (or when it has been selected for a few seconds, anyway), it becomes marked as read and is no longer bold.

If you want to mark a lot of messages as "read" at once, select them and choose Edit, Mark as Read. Or to mark the entire list as read, choose Edit, Mark All Read. You can also do this with the shortcut menu (right-click).

One good reason to mark messages as read is to prevent them from showing up the next time you view the newsgroup. To choose whether or not read messages will show up next time you open this group, choose View, Current View, Hide Read Messages or Show All Messages.

Replying to a Newsgroup Message

You can reply to a newsgroup message publicly or privately. Usually it is considered good manners to reply publicly so everyone can benefit from your information. However, if you have something negative and personal to say to the poster, reply to the individual instead.

To reply publicly, click the Reply Group button. A message composition window appears, with the complete text of the message quoted. You might want to delete some of the lines, to avoid making your reply overly long, but keep any lines that are relevant to your reply. Then compose your reply and click Send. Figure 5.31 shows a reply being composed.

CAUTION Remember, newsgroups are public. A good rule is: Don't write anything that you would be embarrassed to hear on TV as attributed to you.

To reply privately using e-mail, click the Reply button. Compose your e-mail and click Send.

Type your reply here

> signs set off the original material being quoted

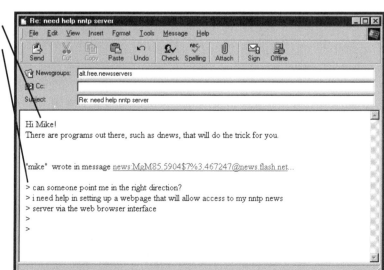

Figure 5.31

A public reply to a public newsgroup posting

Posting a New Message

To post a new message to a newsgroup, first display that newsgroup, and then click the New Post button on the toolbar. Then simply fill in the subject and message, as you do with an e-mail, and click Send. You don't specify a recipient; that information is already filled in based on the newsgroup that was active when you clicked New Post.

Tracking Newsgroup Conversations

If you want to check back to see whether a reply has been posted to a public message in a newsgroup, you can mark it for tracking. That way the message and all the replies to it will appear in red, where it's easier to find.

To do so, choose Message, Watch Conversation, or just click in the Watch column (the one with the eyeglasses in the heading). A symbol appears in the Flag column in the newsgroup listing, and you can sort by that column the next time you view the newsgroup to see all your flagged messages first. For example, Figure 5.32 shows a watched conversation.

To "unwatch" the conversation, click its symbol in the Watch column to turn off the watch indicator. When you click once, the symbol changes to

Watch column

Watch Conversation symbol

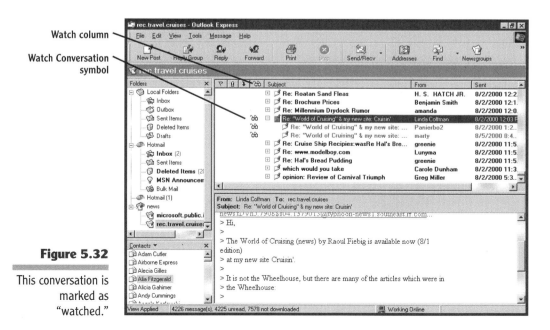

Figure 5.32

This conversation is marked as "watched."

a circle with a red line through it, which means "Ignore Conversation." Click it again to clear all indicators.

Wrapping Up

You can probably find enough to keep you occupied and fascinated all day long on the Internet, but let's keep moving. In this afternoon's session, I show you some miscellaneous tricks and skills that might come in handy, if not specifically this weekend then sometime soon as you work with your PC.

More Fun Things to Try

- ✿ Working with Fonts
- ✿ Checking Out System Information and Exploring the Device Manager
- ✿ Making an Extra Startup Disk
- ✿ Configuring the PC for Multiple Users and Setting Up a Home Network
- ✿ Playing Online Games
- ✿ Researching a Topic and Shopping Online
- ✿ Setting Up a Web Site

This chapter is all about exploring and having fun in Windows Me. You don't do that nearly enough as an adult, do you? In this chapter, I show you a smorgasbord of intermediate-level activities and features that I think are interesting in Windows Me. These are all things that, the first time I saw them, made me think "Oh, how cool!" I hope you get as big a kick out of them as I did.

Working with Fonts

As you learned back in Friday Night's session, a font is a style of lettering, sometimes called a *typeface*. Windows comes with a modest selection of fonts that you can use in formatting your data files in various programs, and when you install other programs, such as Microsoft Office, you get additional fonts too. The more fonts you have, the more fun you can have with typography in your documents.

Viewing Installed Fonts

To check out what fonts you have installed already, do the following:

1. Choose Start, Settings, Control Panel.

2. Double-click Fonts. The installed fonts appear in a folder window with each font represented by an icon.

3. Double-click a font to see a sample of it. Figure 6.1 shows one.

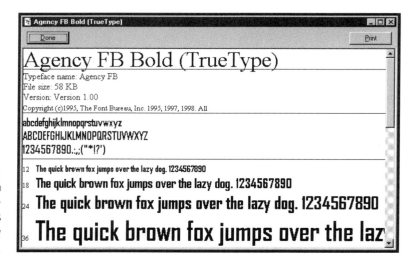

Figure 6.1

When you double-click a font, it opens in a sample window like this one.

4. When you are finished looking at the sample, click Done to close the font's sample window.

There are two kinds of fonts you'll see in the Fonts folder: TrueType fonts and everything else. TrueType fonts have a blue TT on their icon; all other fonts have a red A there. TrueType fonts are designed specifically to work well in Windows and on Macintosh computers and have many advantages, including scalability (that is, you can use them at any size) and the flexibility to work with any printer. The other fonts on your system might include printer-resident fonts and fonts used by Windows itself, but for your purposes, you can lump them all into the category of "everything else."

CAUTION Do not delete the fonts MS Serif and MS Sans Serif from your system. These are fonts Windows uses, and if you delete them, text on menus and in dialog boxes might not display correctly.

The Fonts window is much like any other file-management window that you learned about in Friday Evening's session, but there are a couple of additional features you might want to play around with:

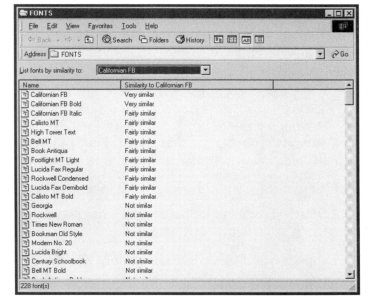

Figure 6.2

The Fonts window enables you to sort the fonts by similarity to a chosen font.

⚙ Choose View, List Fonts by Similarity to display the fonts as shown in Figure 6.2. You can open the List fonts by similarity to drop-down list and click one of the fonts, and then all the other fonts appear in order based on how similar to the chosen font they are. You can use this to delete fonts that are essentially duplicates of some other installed font to save space on your hard disk.

⚙ Choose View, Hide Variations to hide any fonts that are bold or italic versions of some other font. This cuts down on the number of fonts to wade through on the list.

Adding and Removing Fonts

To remove a font, select it and press Delete, just as you do any other file on your PC. All the other deletion methods also work too, such as the Delete button on the toolbar and dragging the item to the Recycle Bin.

You can also add fonts. You might buy a disk of fonts, for example, or download a font for free from the Internet.

CAUTION Many Windows-based programs display only TrueType fonts when they present a list of fonts from which to choose, so when acquiring new fonts, make sure they are of the TrueType variety.

When you buy a disk of fonts, it sometimes comes with its own installation program, and you can use that if you want. But you can also add fonts using Windows' own Add Font utility, as in the following steps:

1. From the Control Panel, double-click the Fonts icon.

2. In the Fonts window, choose File, Install New Font. The Add Fonts dialog box opens.

3. Open the Drives list and choose the drive on which the new font resides.

4. Use the Folders pane to navigate to the folder containing the font. A list of the fonts in that location appears in the List of fonts area. See Figure 6.3.

5. Select the font(s) you want to install from that location. Hold down Ctrl to select more than one at once.

6. (Optional) If you want Windows to use the fonts from their current location rather than copying them to your hard disk, clear the Copy fonts to Fonts folder check box.

Figure 6.3

Navigate to the location of the fonts to be installed, and then choose the font(s) you want to install.

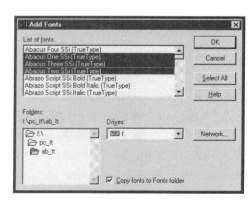

◆ ◆

CAUTION You should copy the fonts to the Fonts folder if the source disk will not always be available (for example, if it's on a CD or floppy or on a network drive that might not always be active).

◆ ◆

7. Click OK. The fonts are added to your Fonts folder.

There are hundreds, even thousands, of fonts available online, and most of them are free. Here are some Web sites that have fonts:

- **Microsoft Typography.** http://www.microsoft.com/typography/default.asp

- **Divide By Zero Fonts.** http://fonts.tom7.com

- **Kemosabe's Font Source.** http://www.fontaddict.com

- **TrueType Typography.** http://www.truetype.demon.co.uk

- **ShyFonts Type Foundry.** http://www.shyfonts.com

Checking Out System Information

Windows Me comes with a great utility called System Information that tells you more than you ever wanted to know about your hardware and software. It's mostly a geek tool, useful for troubleshooting, but ordinary folks might like to explore it just out of general curiosity.

To open System Information, choose Start, Programs, Accessories, System Tools, System Information. A Help and Support window opens with your system information displayed. See Figure 6.4.

The initial screen shown in Figure 6.4 is a System Summary, reporting your operating system version, your processor type, the amount of memory installed, and so on. This information will come in handy when some geek friend asks you what kind of computer you have—you can spout off the processor type and speed and amount of memory, and he or she will be duly impressed. You might also need this information when talking on the phone with a technical support person who is trying to help you trouble-shoot problems with a device.

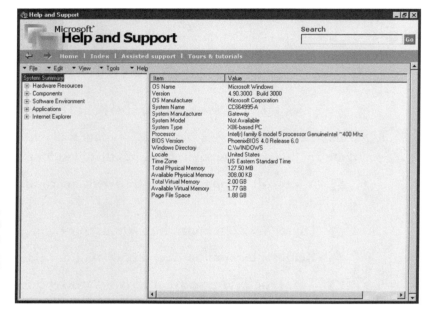

Figure 6.4

System Information tells you what you have in the way of hardware and software.

You can click the other categories in the folder tree to the left of the main window to see other information. I won't belabor every single category here, but here are a few of the more useful ones:

- **Hardware Resources, Conflicts/Sharing.** Shows you which devices are sharing system resources, if any. See Figure 6.5. This can be used to troubleshoot resource conflicts with memory, IRQs, or DMA channels. Sharing does not always mean conflict; some devices, particularly PCI ones, can share without a problem. However, you can use the list as a starting place for troubleshooting. See Appendix A, "Troubleshooting Problems," for more details.

- **Components, Problem Devices.** Shows you any devices that are reporting problems, along with the error code the device is supplying if any. Again, a useful troubleshooting tool.

- **Software Environment, Running Tasks.** A list of everything that's running in Windows at the moment, including all programs that run silently in the background. This list can come as a real shock, because

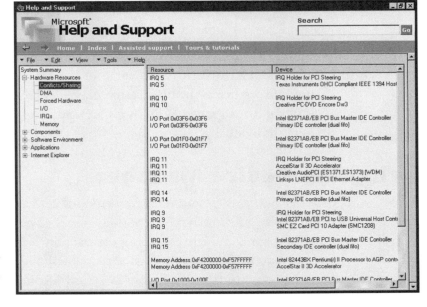

Figure 6.5

System Information reports what resources are being shared by two or more devices or drivers.

it's rather long even when you don't think anything is running. It's useful to see what's running when you are trying to figure out, for example, why ScanDisk or Disk Defragmenter keeps restarting.

Besides all the technical specs provided in System Information, there is also a whole menu of interesting system tools. Open the Tools menu to choose from the list. Here are some of the highlights:

○ **Network Diagnostics.** Displays information about your current network connections, to help troubleshoot problems with them.

○ **Registry Checker.** Checks the system Registry for errors, inconsistencies, and problems. Windows checks the Registry each time it starts up, but this is a more thorough test.

○ **Dr. Watson.** A troubleshooting utility. You turn it on, and it runs in the background as you work. Then when a program crashes or freezes, Dr. Watson records information about the crash that can be used by a technician to diagnose and repair the problem. You can also click the Dr. Watson icon in the System Tray (it appears there when you

start it from the Tools menu) to generate a report of what might be wrong with your system and how you can fix it.

⚙ **System Configuration Utility.** Another name for this program is MSCONFIG, which is the name of the file that runs it. (You've used this earlier in the book, remember?) It shows you exactly what is being loaded when Windows starts, and lets you disable certain items individually.

Exploring the Device Manager

The Device Manager is another great behind-the-scenes tool for examining your system. It shows you the various pieces of hardware attached to your motherboard, and lets you configure each one's settings. You'll work with it extensively if you go through the troubleshooting in Appendix A, but I'll take you through a quick tour of it now just for fun.

To open Device Manager, right-click My Computer and choose Properties, and then click the Device Manager tab. The Device Manager lists various categories of devices; click the plus sign next to a category to see the individual devices you have in that category. For example, Figure 6.6 shows the Device Manager with the CD-ROM category expanded.

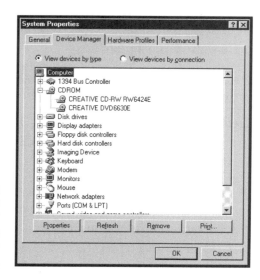

Figure 6.6

Device Manager provides an overview of your hardware.

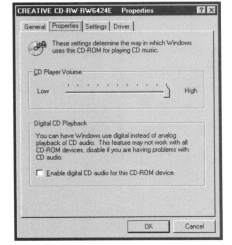

Figure 6.7

Figure 6.7

Each device has its own Properties tab.

To check out a device's properties, double-click it. For example, Figure 6.7 shows the properties for my rewritable CD-ROM drive. Most have multiple tabs; the Properties tab appears in Figure 6.7.

CAUTION ◆
Don't make changes to a device's properties unless you have a specific reason for doing so, and even then, be sure you know what you're doing.
◆ ◆

Also in the Device Manager you can get a quick look at the system resources being used (IRQs, DMA channels, and so on). Just double-click the Computer icon at the top of the Device Manager tree to open a dialog box with all that information. Don't worry if you don't know what an IRQ or a DMA channel is; they are covered in Appendix A.

Making an Extra Startup Disk

When you installed Windows Me, the setup program prompted you to create a startup disk (a.k.a. an *Emergency Boot Disk*). This process created a floppy disk that you can use to start your PC if something bad happens to it that prevents it from starting normally.

NOTE   The startup disk contains the files Io.sys and Command.com, which are needed to start the computer and display a command prompt at which you can type text commands. It also contains a utility that creates a temporary "virtual disk" out of a few megabytes of your system's memory, and copies some utilities onto it that are useful when troubleshooting a system.

If you didn't install Windows Me (perhaps it came pre-installed?) or if you have misplaced your startup disk, you should make another one. Better safe than sorry.

To create a startup disk, follow these steps:

1. Choose Start, Settings, Control Panel.

2. Double-click Add/Remove Programs.

3. Click the Startup Disk tab (see Figure 6.8).

4. Insert a blank floppy disk (or one that contains nothing you want to keep).

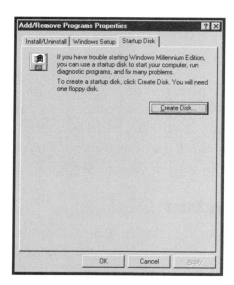

Figure 6.8

There's only one thing you can do on the Startup Disk tab: Create Disk.

5. Click Create Disk.

6. A message appears prompting you to insert the disk; click OK.

7. Wait for the needed files to be copied to the floppy.

8. When the Copy Progress box goes away, the disk is finished. Remove it from the drive and click OK to close the Add/Remove Programs Properties dialog box.

After you've gone to the trouble of making the disk, store it somewhere safe. If you ever have problems starting your PC, you will appreciate the fact that you have it.

Configuring the PC for Multiple Users

If several people in your household share the computer, there is probably an ongoing battle for who will control the Windows settings such as color scheme, font size, screen saver, and desktop shortcuts. First one person changes an item, and then someone else sits down and changes it back, and nobody is happy. It's like having to share the radio preset buttons in the car.

Fortunately, you can set up Windows Me so that each person has individual settings. Each time you start Windows, you log in, and depending on who logs in, different settings are loaded.

CAUTION Windows Me doesn't have any user-level security in its login process. Anyone can log in, enter a new name and password, and be added to the PC's user list. If you need more security, you might want to look at Windows 2000, which is more network-aware and has more security features.

Enabling Multiuser Operation

To set up Windows Me for multiple users, you must enable the User profiles feature. This makes Windows keep track of separate desktop and Start menu settings for each user.

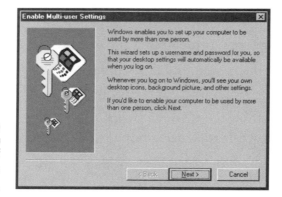

Figure 6.9

You'll see this if multiple users are not already set up.

1. Choose Start, Settings, Control Panel and double-click Users. The Enable Multi-user Settings Wizard runs.

   If it doesn't run, user profiles are already turned on for this PC; you can skip the rest of the steps.

2. Click Next. The Enable Multi-user Settings dialog box opens. See Figure 6.9.

3. Type a username to set up, and click Next.

4. Type a password for that user in the Enter New Password box, and then again in the Confirm password box. Then click Next. If you leave both boxes blank, there will be no password for that user.

5. On the list that appears (see Figure 6.10), place a check mark next to each item that you want to personalize for this user.

Figure 6.10

Specify which settings should be customizable for this user.

6. Choose how the user settings should be managed:

   ✪ Choose Create copies of the current items and their content to duplicate all the chosen items on the list (step 6) for each user you create. I recommend you choose this if you are not sure.

   ✪ Choose Create new items to save disk space to reduce the amount of hard disk space consumed by the feature. This creates new folders only for user content that differs from the default.

CAUTION   If you choose Start Menu from the list in step 5, and you choose Create new items to save disk space in step 6, your Start menu will be nearly empty, and you will not have access to any of the programs that are already installed on your system. Therefore, if you are planning to have a customized Start menu for each user, make sure you choose Create copies of the current items and their content in step 6.

7. Click Next to continue, and then click Finish.

8. When prompted to restart Windows, click Yes.

9. At the login box, type your username (or select it from a list if available) and password (if you're using one) and click OK. You are now logged in as yourself, and you are ready to set up other users.

Adding Other Users

After the initial setup that you went through in the preceding section, you will probably want to add other users. To do so, revisit Users Properties from the Control Panel. This time, instead of the Wizard running, a User Settings dialog box appears, as shown in Figure 6.11.

From here, click New User. The Add User dialog box appears. Click Next, and then work through the setup for this user, the same as you did in the preceding steps.

You also can create a new user by copying the settings from an existing one. To do so, from the Users list select the user to copy and then click Make a

Figure 6.11

Add users and manage the settings for existing ones here.

Copy. The Add User Wizard starts, the same as in the preceding steps, except that the default settings are the ones from the user you are copying.

New users also can set themselves up, unless you are on a network where that has been prevented. If you type a new name in the User box when Windows starts up, Windows Networking will detect that this is a new person and will ask the following:

```
You have not logged on at this computer before. Would you
like this computer to retain your individual settings for use
when you log on here in the future?
```

Click Yes to set up that person as a new user on-the-fly. Choosing No allows the person to log in to Windows but does not retain any of her settings.

Now that you have some user profiles set up, you can customize your Windows environment freely, confident that nobody else will have to put up with your choice in color schemes or your menu arrangement. The following sections explain how to use and configure a multiuser Windows PC.

Switching Between Users

Each time Windows starts, you are prompted to log in to Windows by providing your username and password. That's how Windows determines whose settings to load.

To change users without restarting the PC, choose Start, Log Off name, where name is the person currently logged in. The Log Off Windows box appears; click Yes. Then log in as another user.

Deleting a User

When you delete a user, Windows deletes all the customized settings for that user. Because the settings for each user take up disk space, it is good housekeeping to delete any users who will no longer be using your PC.

To delete a user, go back to the User Properties dialog box (via the Users icon in the Control Panel). Click the user you want to delete, click the Delete button, and click Yes.

Changing a User's Settings

The settings that you specify when you create a user are merely a starting point; you can change them at any time. For example, you might decide that users should not have separate Favorites folders and want to disable personalized settings for that item for each user. Or, you might decide that you don't want separate copies of everything for each user taking up space on your hard disk.

To change the settings, go back to the User Properties dialog box (from the Users icon in the Control Panel) and then do the following:

1. Select the user whose settings you want to change.

2. Click Change Settings. The Personalized Items Settings dialog box opens. (It has the same options as the box you saw in Figure 6.10.)

3. Select or deselect items to be personalized.

4. Choose how you want them personalized (Create copies of the current items and their content or Create new items to save disk space).

5. Click OK.

Turning Off Multiuser Operation

If you stop sharing your PC with others, you might want to disable the multiuser capability. This can save time because you won't be faced with

a login box every time you start Windows (provided you have not set a Windows login password).

Turning off multiuser operation does not delete the user profiles that you might have set up, or any settings from those profiles. It simply stops using them and reverts to the original settings that were in place before you turned on multiuser operation. If you later re-enable multiuser operation, all the former users will reappear in the User Settings dialog box's user list.

To turn off multiuser operation:

1. Choose Start, Settings, Control Panel and double-click Passwords.

2. Click the User Profiles tab.

3. Choose All users of this computer use the same preferences and desktop settings.

4. Click OK.

5. When prompted to restart your computer, click Yes.

Setting Up a Home Network

Earlier versions of Windows were difficult to set up for networking (for the average non-technical person, that is!), but Windows Me makes it simple. Anyone can set up a home network without any special expertise.

Why would you want a network? Well, for one thing it makes it a lot easier to exchange files among the PCs. You can also play multi-player games on your home network, share printers, and even share an Internet connection.

Hardware Needed for Home Networking

You can buy several types of networking kits at your local computer or office supply store. Some of these use telephone lines in your home to network; others use wireless infrared. But the most popular type of network is an Ethernet network, so that's the type I focus on here.

There are also several kinds of networks. The big corporate kind employs a *server*, a PC dedicated to the task of managing the traffic among the other

PCs and providing access to files and printers. But in a home environment, you probably don't have an extra PC to spare for a server, so you will likely want to set up a peer-to-peer network. Such networks simply connect several PCs together, with all the PCs being equals, or *peers.*

In a peer-to-peer Ethernet network, each PC has a network card, which fits into a slot in the motherboard. You plug a network cable into the card, and then run the cables from each PC to a *network hub,* a little box that directs the traffic between them. Many networking kits you can buy in stores contain two network cards, a hub, and the needed cabling.

Setting Up a PC for Networking

First you install the network cards in each PC. Then you run the cabling and plug in the power to the hub. Then you run the Home Networking Wizard on each PC to install the software that Windows needs to let that PC participate in the network.

The Home Networking Wizard automates the task of installing the correct drivers and protocols needed for network operation. It can also set you up to share an Internet connection on one PC with all the others in the network.

Run the Home Networking Wizard by doing the following:

1. Choose Start, Programs, Accessories, Communications, Home Networking Wizard. Then click Next to begin.

    First it asks about your Internet connection. See Figure 6.12. It asks this because Internet connection sharing can be enabled at the same time you set up the home networking (as you'll see in step 3).

2. If this computer has no Internet connection, choose No, this computer does not use the Internet, click Next, and go on to step 4.

    Otherwise, do the following:

    A. Choose Yes, this computer uses the following.

    B. If this computer gets its Internet access through an existing Internet Connection Sharing setup, choose A connection to another computer....

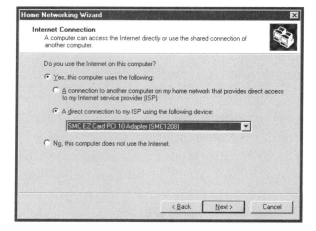

Figure 6.12

Enter information about this PC's Internet connection.

> **C.** If this computer has its own Internet access, choose A direct connection to my ISP using the following device, and then open the drop-down list and choose your Internet connection device. It might be a dial-up networking connection, or it might be a network card (if you have cable or DSL access).
>
> **D.** Click Next to continue.

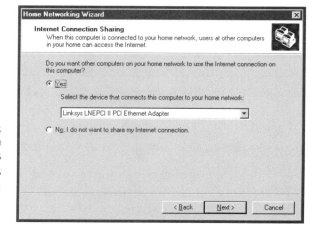

Figure 6.13

Specify whether this PC will share its Internet connection with other PCs in your home.

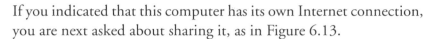

If you indicated that this computer has its own Internet connection, you are next asked about sharing it, as in Figure 6.13.

3. To share your Internet connection with other PCs in your home network, choose Yes, and then open the drop-down list and choose the network card that connects you to the home network. Otherwise choose No. Then click Next.

4. Enter a computer name by which this computer will be known on your home network in the Computer Name box.

5. In the Workgroup Name area, leave the default workgroup name selected, or click the Use this workgroup name option button and enter a workgroup name to use. See Figure 6.14. Then click Next.

◆ ◆

CAUTION If your Internet access involves a network card, such as with a cable modem, the Computer Name and Workgroup Name should not be changed. Leave them at their current settings. For example, my cable Internet provider requires that my Workgroup Name be set to @HOME.

◆ ◆

6. If you want to share your My Documents folder on the network, mark the My Documents folder and all folders in it check box.

Figure 6.14

Choose a PC name and Workgroup name, or leave the defaults.

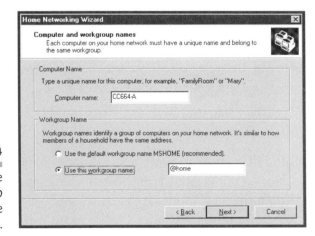

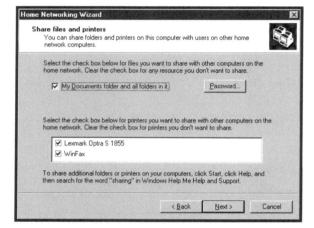

Figure 6.15

Choose what you
want to share from
this PC.

If you want to add a password for sharing, so that only those who know
the password can use the files, click the Password button to set that up.

7. If you want to share your printer with other PCs on the network,
   leave the check mark next to the printer name; otherwise remove it.
   See Figure 6.15. Then click Next.

NOTE You can share other drives and folders besides My Documents; you can set that up later
in Windows Explorer or My Computer by right-clicking on a drive or folder and using the
Sharing tab in its Properties box.

8. If you did not specify a password in step 6, a message box appears
   suggesting that you do so. You can click the Password button to do
   so, or click Next again to move on without it.

   You're asked whether you want to create a Home Networking
   Setup disk.

9. If all the PCs on your home network have Windows Me installed,
   click No, do not create a Home Networking setup disk; click Next,
   and skip to step 11. (You can run the Home Networking Wizard on
   any other Windows Me PCs to set them up without a disk.)

On the other hand, if you have PCs on your home network that do not use Windows Me, choose Yes, create a Home Networking disk and click Next, and then go on to step 10.

10. Insert a blank disk (or one containing nothing you want to keep), and click Next and wait for the needed files to be copied to the floppy disk.

11. At the Completing the Home Network Wizard screen, click the Finish button.

12. When asked whether you want to restart your PC now, remove the floppy disk from your drive (if you created a Home Networking disk) and then click Yes.

13. When the computer restarts, a message appears that home networking is set up; click OK.

Sharing an Internet Connection

As you just saw, the Home Networking Wizard sets up your Internet connection sharing automatically. Even if you already have a home network, you can run the Home Networking Wizard to configure your PC for Internet sharing.

You can set up Internet Connection Sharing manually by adding the Internet Connection Sharing component in Windows with Add/Remove Programs (covered at the beginning of Saturday Morning). It's not a different method, though, because when you restart the PC, the Home Networking Wizard runs just as it does if you had chosen it from the Start menu and gone the other route.

Working with Network Drives and Printers

You can use network drives and printers the same way you use local ones on your own hard disk. Most Windows-based programs allow you to browse the network when choosing a location for opening or saving files. For example, in Figure 6.16, Word 2000's Open dialog box shows a network drive being browsed.

Figure 6.16

You browse the network the same as you browse a drive.

To use a shared network printer, select it from the Print dialog box. Most Windows programs have a Printer drop-down list; any network printer installed will appear there.

If the network printer doesn't appear on that list, use the Add Printer Wizard (Start, Printers) to set it up. As you are setting up a printer with this Wizard, it will ask you whether it is a network or local printer. Choose Network, and browse the network to find it. The Wizard will then copy the needed drivers from the host PC to your own, so that you can print to that printer as seamlessly as to your own local one.

Sharing Your Own Drives and Printers

Networking is not necessarily a two-way street; just because you can access other people's printers and drives does not automatically mean they can access yours. You must set up your PC to specifically share your resources.

First, enable file and printer sharing by doing the following. (If you chose to share your my Documents folder or any of your printers when you ran the Home Networking Wizard, file and printer sharing is already turned on and you can skip this.)

1. Choose Start, Settings, Control Panel and double-click Network.

2. Click the File and Print Sharing button.

Figure 6.17

File and Print
Sharing must be
turned on before
you can share
anything on your
home network.

3. Make sure that both check boxes are marked in the dialog box that appears (see Figure 6.17); then click OK.

4. Click Close to close the Network dialog box. If prompted to restart your PC, choose Yes to do so.

Once file and printer sharing is enabled, you can right-click a printer (in the Printers folder) or a drive or folder (in My Computer) and choose Sharing from its shortcut menu; then choose Share As and enter a share name for it. See Figure 6.18. This makes that particular resource available for others. You can share it as Read-Only, Full, or Depends on Password. Full grants all others permission to add, modify, and delete; Depends on Password does too but asks them for a password first, so you can keep everyone out except a select group of users.

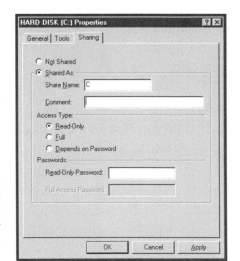

Figure 6.18

You can share
drives, folders, or
printers by turning
on sharing for them.

If you have a cable Internet connection , you should definitely use a password for file sharing. Otherwise, someone could use the Internet to access your PC and view, modify, or even delete important files.

Using CD-RW and DVD Drives

This section talks about some of the fun you can have with multimedia devices like DVD and CD-RW drives. Not everyone has this equipment, of course, but more and more new systems these days are coming with such devices. Even if you don't have some of this stuff, you might still want to read the following sections—they might even make you decide to buy some new hardware!

Playing a DVD Movie

DVD stands for Digital Versatile Disk, and it's the latest thing in CD-ROMs. A DVD disk is like a super CD; it holds lots more data. How much? Enough for over two hours of full-motion video footage. That's why the primary use of DVDs right now is to store and play movies. DVDs can also hold computer data too, but that usage is still in its infancy. Expect to see more and more of it in the coming years, though.

If you have a DVD drive on your PC, it functions just like a regular CD-ROM drive in most respects, all by itself. However, if you want to play DVD disks in that drive, you need an MPEG decoder card hooked up to it. Most DVD drives these days come with an MPEG card, but on some newer systems the video card serves as the MPEG card. You might also need to install some DVD software that comes with the card or the drive.

If you have all the right hardware in place, and the drivers installed, you can simply pop a DVD disk in the drive and it starts playing.

If your video card supports DVD playback, the Windows DVD player can play your DVD movies. You'll find it on the Accessories menu if your hardware is compatible with it. But your DVD drive itself probably came with a DVD player of its own, so if you don't find the Windows DVD player on the menu, go with the player designed specifically for your equipment. For example, I have a Creative PC-DVD drive with its own MPEG

decoder card, and Windows DVD Player won't work with it, but it plays movies just fine with the Creative DVD player it came with.

Besides movies, you can also play DVD data disks on your DVD drive. These are not that common yet, but some games are beginning to be released on DVD disks. For graphic-intensive games this is a plus, because you don't have to swap CDs in the middle of the game.

Making Your Own CD-ROMs

If you have a writable or rewritable CD-ROM drive, you can make your own CD-ROMs.

The original units could write to a blank CD only once; then that blank was permanently written, and nothing could be added, changed, or removed. Those are *CD-Recordable* (CD-R) drives. Newer ones can do the CD-R thing, but can also write to a different kind of disk, *CD-Rewritable* (CD-RW), which can be changed and erased multiple times. The CD-RW blanks are more expensive, so most people who want to make a CD that won't change use the cheaper CD-R blanks.

Your CD-R or CD-RW drive came with software for making your own CDs; Windows itself doesn't have an application to do that. There are two separate programs—one for CD-R disks and one for CD-RW. One popular CD-R program is Easy CDCreator by Adaptec. A limited-functionality version of it comes free with most CD-R and CD-RW drives. Another one is called Nero Burning ROM.

A separate program handles transfer of files to a CD-RW drive using a technology called *packet writing*. This enables you to use the CD-RW disk as if it were a floppy disk, dragging-and-dropping files to it using Windows Explorer or My Computer.

Making LPs and Cassettes into Audio CDs

If you have a CD-R or CD-RW drive and a sound card with a Line In jack, you can turn your old LPs and cassettes into audio CDs. Some CD-R programs come with software that makes this easy, but even if yours doesn't, you can still do it. The basic process is this: you hook up your stereo system so

Figure 6.19

You can use Sound Recorder if you don't have any other, more sophisticated, programs for recording incoming analog music.

that the Line Out goes to the Line In on your sound card. At that point you should be able to hear the stereo play through your computer's speakers. Then you use a program that records sound (such as Sound Recorder, which comes with Windows) to record the stereo playing as a WAV file. Then you use your CD-R program to turn the WAV files into an audio CD.

NOTE The Sound Recorder program is at Start, Programs, Accessories, Entertainment, Sound Recorder. It is simple, and works just like a tape recorder. See Figure 6.19.

If you are serious about transferring a lot of LPs and cassettes to CD format, you might want to invest in software that can help you remove some of the pops, hisses, and scratches from the original recordings. Adaptec's Easy CD Creator Deluxe does this, and several other programs are available that do it too. Such programs take the place of Sound Recorder, and record the input while running it through a filter that improves the quality.

Backing Up Important Files to CD-R or CD-RW

CD-R and CD-RW disks make excellent backup devices. You can periodically copy your important files to a CD-R or CD-RW disk, in case disaster strikes and your hard disk contents become destroyed.

Windows 98 came with a backup program, but Windows Me does not. However, there are many good backup programs available for sale in stores, and you can always simply copy the files from your hard disk to a CD-RW drive using Windows Explorer, or periodically create a CD-R containing your most important data files.

One little glitch is that when you copy files, or back them up with a backup program, most hidden and system files are not included, and some of these are essential for your Windows system to operate. So even if you have done what you thought was a complete backup, you might not be able to perfectly restore your hard disk from the backup. The solution? Use a hard disk copying program such as DriveImage or Norton Ghost. Such programs create an exact duplicate of your hard disk on one or more CD-R or CD-RW disks, and provide a utility for restoring from the backup when needed. Such programs work with both CD-R and CD-RW drives, as well as Zip drives, Jaz drives, tape backup drives, and other removable media.

Playing Online Games

Playing computer games is no longer necessarily a solitary activity. Many of the most popular computer games these days have an online feature that lets you play the game with other people, either on the Internet, on your home network, or both. (Each PC that participates must have its own copy of the game.) Check the directions for a specific game to find out how to set it up.

Windows Me comes with several games designed specifically for playing online through Microsoft's MSN Zone. Participation is free and anonymous. The games include Backgammon, Checkers, Hearts, Reversi, and Spades, and all are accessible on the Games menu.

To try one out (Backgammon, in this case), follow these steps:

1. Establish your Internet connection if you are not already connected. (Sunday Morning explained how.)

2. Choose Start, Programs, Games, Internet Backgammon. An introduction box appears; click Play.

3. Wait for the service to match you up with another player. When it does, the Backgammon board appears. See Figure 6.20.

Microsoft offers even more free games at the MSN Zone (http://www.zone.com). These are accessible to everyone, not just Windows Me users. To play one of the free games here, just click the game you want, choose a "room" to play in, and you're off. Rooms in the MSN Zone are groups of players with

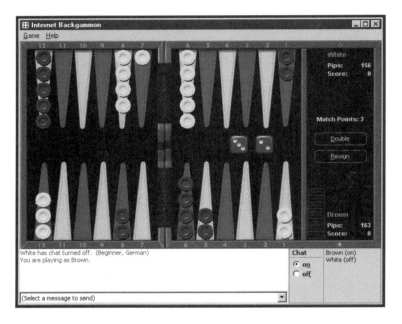

Figure 6.20

It's just like playing a regular computer game, except your opponent is a live person somewhere on the Internet.

common goals. There are social rooms where the gameplay is relaxed and "for fun," and competitive rooms where your opponents are out for blood.

The first time you choose a game, a message might appear saying that you do not have the needed software and offering to download it for you. Click Yes, and follow the prompts. To download software, you must be a Zone member. It's free, but you must choose a user ID and password and enter your e-mail address. After registering, you can download the needed software.

When you go to a game, the MSN Gaming Zone login box appears, as shown in Figure 6.21. Log in using the user ID and password you created, and you're taken to a "zone" where you can play a game.

Figure 6.22 shows a cribbage zone called Town Square. To participate in a game, click one of the empty chairs to "sit down" at that table, and the game begins automatically.

Once the game starts, the game play is similar to an offline game program that you might play.

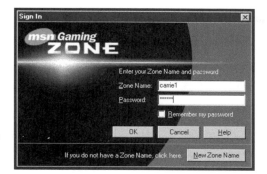

Figure 6.21

The login for the MSN Gaming Zone

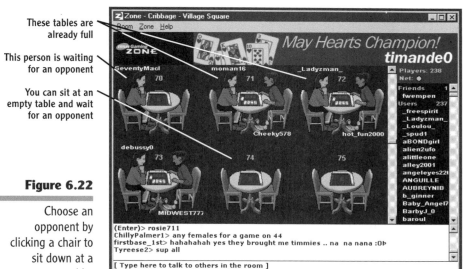

These tables are already full

This person is waiting for an opponent

You can sit at an empty table and wait for an opponent

Figure 6.22

Choose an opponent by clicking a chair to sit down at a game table.

Microsoft is far from the only company to offer free online games; here are some other sites to check out:

⚙ **I Win.** http://www.iwin.com

⚙ **The Belly.** http://www.thebelly.com

⚙ **Pogo.** http://www.pogo.com

⚙ **Mplayer.** http://www.mplayer.com

⚙ **Free Arcade.** http://www.freearcade.com

⚙ **Uproar.** http://www.uproar.com

Researching a Topic Online

If you ask people why they want Internet access, one of the most common reasons given is "to do research." But what exactly do people research once they get there? There are thousands of answers. Here are some of the more common research topics, along with some ideas of where to find the information sought.

Researching a Product or Service Online

You can use the Web to get information about nearly any product or service before you buy it. It seems like every product's manufacturer has a Web site these days.

If you want information about a particular brand, start with that company's Web site. You can try to guess the address by trying the obvious (http://www.*companyname*.com), or look up the company's name at a search site such as Yahoo (http://www.yahoo.com). Then when you get to the company site, look for a Product Information section for specs on the product.

For consumer reviews, try Consumer Reports at http://www.consumerreports.org. There is also a nice selection of reviews of products at http://www.superpages.com/cr.

If you are shopping for a new vehicle, try CarPoint (http://www.carpoint.com) or AutoVantage (http://www.autovantage.com). Both can tell you the invoice price for a given vehicle and help you price it with options, arrange financing, and lots more. For example, in Figure 6.23, I'm shopping for a new Chevrolet Prizm.

Doing Research for School Papers

If you have kids in K-12, they probably have to write the occasional research paper. (And if you're in college or graduate school, academic research is probably a big chunk of your life!) The Internet makes academic research a lot less painful.

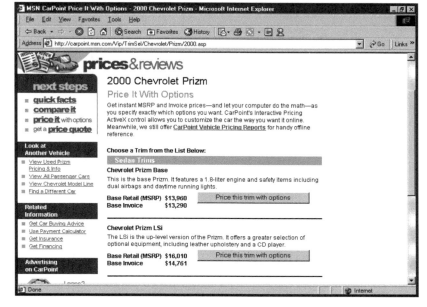

Figure 6.23

CarPoint offers tons of free information about new and used cars.

There are many online encyclopedias available, and this is often a good place to start the research. These typically have a few paragraphs of information on whatever topic you're looking for, with links to more information available elsewhere. Some of the top online encyclopedias are:

- **Compton's Home Library.** http://www.comptons.com
- **World Book Encyclopedia.** http://www.worldbook.com
- **Encyclopedia Britannica.** http://www.britannica.com
- **Microsoft Encarta.** http://www.encarta.com
- **Funk and Wagnalls.** http://www.funkandwagnalls.com

And here are some other, non-encyclopedia links to check out too for K-12 research papers:

- **ResearchPaper.com.** http://www.researchpaper.com
- **Biography.com.** http://www.biography.com
- **Why Files.** http://whyfiles.org/index.html

Getting Online Homework Help

If your kids need help with their schoolwork but you aren't sure of the answer yourself, where do you turn? Fortunately, there are lots of Web sites that specialize in homework help for children, such as:

- **Star Tribune Homework Help.** http://www.startribune.com/education/homework.shtml

- **BrainMania.** http://www.brainmania.com

- **Homework Help Links.** http://www.albedo.net/~arvic/homework.html

- **Ask an Expert**. http://njnie.dl.stevens-tech.edu/askanexpert.html

Finding General Reference Information Online

You don't have to be a student to occasionally need help remembering all those little survival factoids you should have learned in school. Whether it's the spelling of a particular word you're looking for or help converting fractions to decimals, you can count on the following sites:

- **The American Heritage Book of English Usage.** http://www.bartleby.com/64/

- **Bartlett's Familiar Quotations.** http://www.bartleby.com/99/

- **Library of Congress.** http://www.loc.gov/

- **One Across (Crossword Puzzle Dictionary).** http://www.oneacross.com

- **Information Please.** http://www.infoplease.com

- **Alternative Dictionaries of International Slang.** http://www.notam.uio.no/~hcholm/altlang

- **All Experts.** http://www.allexperts.com

- ⚙ **Acronym Finder.** http://www.acronymfinder.com
- ⚙ **Babelfish (translator).** http://babelfish.altavista.com/translate.dyn

And that's just the tip of the iceberg.

Shopping Online

If you haven't bought anything via the Internet yet, you probably soon will. People everywhere are discovering that the Internet is a rich source of bargains. You won't have to pay retail ever again once you discover the best places to shop online.

Predictably, computing is the biggest-selling category of goods sold online, but you can buy everything from airline tickets to groceries with just a few mouse clicks.

Online Stores

Most online stores offer at least 20 percent off of regular retail prices, on items such as audio CDs, videos, electronics, computer equipment, and books. Such stores are everywhere, but some of the bigger ones include Amazon (http://www.amazon.com), CD-Now (http://www.cdnow.com), and Buy.com (http://www.buy.com).

Price Comparison Sites

Certain Web sites collect the prices from dozens of other sites and let you do side-by-side comparisons for the best values. Two such sites are Computer Shopper (http://www.computershopper.com) and Price Watch (http://www.pricewatch.com). They mainly deal with computers and electronic equipment. For example, in Figure 6.24, I'm shopping for a Palm Vx; ComputerShopper has sorted the list of vendors so that those with the cheapest prices appear first.

Name-Your-Price Sites

These sites let you, the customer, propose a price for a product or service, and your proposition is then accepted or rejected within a certain timeframe. Price Line is the most famous of these (http://www.priceline.com); they originally sold airline travel, but have since branched out into other areas as well such as hotel accommodations and even groceries.

Online Auctions

Auction sites such as Onsale.com revolutionized the online buying experience by conducting online auctions, usually with a 2–3 day duration. You see an item you want, click a button to bid on it, and then check back later to see whether you've been outbid. At the closing of the auction, the high bidder gets the item (usually charged to a credit card). At such sites, the selling party is usually a company that has paid a fee to use the auction system.

Person-to-person auctions are also common. The biggest and best-organized site handling these is ebay (http://www.ebay.com). On these sites, you can

not only buy at auction, but also post your own stuff for sale, complete with pictures.

Setting Up a Web Site

One of the nice parts about the Internet is that it's democratic. Everyone has the opportunity to participate, both in viewing content and in providing it. Case in point: the Web site. Creating your own Web site is not that difficult, and in just a few hours you can be sharing your knowledge and opinions with millions of other people all over the world.

If you're planning to complete this Sunday Afternoon session by suppertime tonight, you'd better postpone your Web site creation plans until another day, because you'll need time to develop and format your content. But I'll quickly run though how it's done, and you can return here later to do the work.

First, you need some server space. Most ISPs give each user a certain amount of free server space, so check to see whether you already have some. (Some ISPs put restrictions on what you can do with it, such as not selling anything and not offering "adult" content.) America Online also offers some server space free to its users. If you don't have any server space, or the restrictions on it make it unsuitable for your plans, you need to get some more. One way is to pay your ISP extra money each month for it; another way is to sign up with a Web hosting company. These companies rent out space on their server to anyone who needs it. Prices usually start at around $20 a month.

Next, you need a Web address that people will type in when they want to visit your Web site. You have a choice. One is to use the regular address of the server. For example, the URL for the free server space your ISP provides might be http://members.myprovider.com/personal/~jdoe99. Obviously that's long and awkward to type. But it's free, and there's no special setup required.

Your other alternative is to get your own domain name (for a $70 upfront fee which covers the first two years). You usually can't use a domain name with free server space, so you'll need to go the Web host route. A domain name is www, and then your domain name, and then an extension (.com is the most common). For example, www.microsoft.com is a domain, as is www.usps.gov and www.gateway.org. (Those are already taken.) When you sign up with a Web host, they will usually help you get a domain name for free (except for the $70 registration fee). You can go to http://domreg.ahnet.net to see what names are already taken.

Finally, you need some content. You can create Web pages in any of a variety of programs. Most Microsoft products can save in Web format, so you can create content in whatever program you are already comfortable with, and then publish it to your Web server space. (Check with your ISP or Web host to find out how to transfer your content to the server.)

I won't get into the nitty-gritty details of content creation here, because it could take up the rest of the book! But if you're interested in learning more, get the book *Create Your First Web Page In a Weekend* by Steve Callihan, and start that project *next* weekend.

NOTE If you have Microsoft Office 2000, it might have come with a program called FrontPage. FrontPage is a Web site creation tool that can help you create some snazzy-looking pages with a minimum of technical know-how. However, to use a Web site created in FrontPage, your Web server must support FrontPage extensions. Check with your ISP or Web host to find out.

Congratulations

Congratulations! You made it to the end of this weekend course. I hope you've learned a lot and had some fun too. The last section of the book, Appendix A, is a troubleshooting guide. You might not need it right away, but keep the book around, because you'll probably need it eventually.

If you have enjoyed this book, and want to learn more, I suggest the following books:

- *Tune Up Your PC In a Weekend,* by Faithe Wempen
- *Upgrade Your PC In a Weekend, Revised Edition* by Faithe Wempen
- *Get Your Family on the Internet In a Weekend,* by Catherine Nelson
- *Learn HTML In a Weekend, 3rd Edition,* by Steve Callihan

Troubleshooting Problems

There's a joke circulating on the Internet to the effect that if Windows were a car, you would have to take it in for repairs every week. Actually that's probably closer to the truth than you might like to believe! Many minor problems can crop up in Windows, and if left unchecked, some of them can turn into major problems.

Fortunately, many of the most common problems are easy to fix. In this appendix, I show you how to solve the most common Windows problems yourself, in many cases saving you an expensive trip to a computer repair shop.

Before you get started here, do two things:

- Turn off your system by choosing Start, Shut Down and selecting Shut Down. Turn off the PC's power if it doesn't turn itself off. Wait 15 seconds, and turn it back on again. This is called a *cold reboot*, and it often corrects minor problems. If you can't shut down normally, turn off the PC's power using its Power button, and then turn it back on again.

⚙ If you can get into Windows at all, check your system for errors using ScanDisk (covered in the Saturday Evening session). I have found that ScanDisk fixes the majority of the problems I have with my system.

Still having problems or can't do either of these things for some reason? Then continue with this appendix.

Do You Have a Virus?

A few years ago I used to tell clients who were worried about computer viruses that they were being paranoid. However, today that is no longer the case. Virus infections are becoming more and more common on average people's PCs, primarily because of the Internet. The capability to exchange files and messages with the whole world also brings the capability for viruses to spread freely.

It's difficult to generalize about the symptoms of virus infection because every virus is different. Some viruses send malicious e-mail; others delete certain files from your PC, or disable it completely.

If you already have a virus protection program, keep it running all the time, and download regular updates to it from the manufacturer's Web site. Two popular antivirus programs are Norton Antivirus (http://www.symantec.com) and McAfee VirusScan (http://www.mcafee.com). Both offer free trial versions for download.

It's also important to keep your virus removal boot disk current. When you installed your antivirus program, it probably instructed you to make a virus-removal boot disk when you installed it. There should also be a command in the program for making another disk, and you should go through that command to make a new boot disk (reusing the same floppy disk) each time you download an update to your virus data files.

If you ever suspect that you have a virus on your system, run the virus scanning portion of your antivirus software from within Windows if possible. If you can't start Windows, boot the system from your virus removal disk, and follow the prompts that appear to check for viruses.

♦ ♦

Before booting from your virus removal disk, make sure it is write-protected. In other words, make sure the little sliding tab in the corner of the disk is open, so you can see through the hole. Otherwise the virus can infect the floppy disk from an infected hard drive.

♦ ♦

If you don't yet have a virus protection program, and therefore don't have a virus removal boot disk, go to a friend's PC who has such a program installed and make a boot disk there using his or her program. (Check the online help for the virus protection program on your friend's PC to find out how.)

The Computer Won't Start

If you can't get Windows to come up at all, that's a pretty serious error. So let's start there, for those unfortunate souls in that position. Bear with me: "Doesn't start" is a broad topic, and I need to ask you to narrow down your problem in the following sections.

Blank Screen

The hardest problems to troubleshoot are those in which you don't see anything at all onscreen.

- **Blank screen, no fan.** The computer is not getting power. Is it plugged in? Is the wall outlet working? If so, perhaps your computer's power supply has gone bad.

- **Blank screen, fan sounds but no disk activity.** A hardware problem exists. This can happen if the hard or floppy disk is not hooked up right (wrong cabling or settings) or if the video card is not functioning or is not firmly seated in its slot. It's rare, but sometimes they do wiggle loose, especially if you have recently moved the computer.

- **Blank screen, multiple beeps.** The memory is not installed right, or there's a problem with your memory or motherboard. One or the other might have gone bad.

✪ **Blank screen, single beep, disk activity.** The computer is starting normally, but the monitor isn't showing it. Is the monitor turned on? Plugged in? Connected to the computer? Contrast and brightness adjusted appropriately?

These are all hardware problems. You can attempt to solve them yourself, or you might consider calling in a techie friend or computer repairperson. If you want to fix things yourself, check out Prima Tech's *Upgrade Your PC In a Weekend* by Faithe Wempen, especially the Sunday Afternoon session on troubleshooting.

Error Message on Black Screen

When you first start the computer, some *BIOS* information (that is, basic input/output system information) appears onscreen. It tells you what video card you have, what processor, and how much memory. This is normal. Then Windows usually starts.

If you see an error message instead of Windows starting, however, here are some hints:

✪ **Floppy disk fail message.** Your floppy drive is bad or is not hooked up right.

✪ **Hard disk fail message.** Your hard disk is bad or is not hooked up right.

✪ **Boot failure message.** Your hard disk can't start Windows. It might be going bad, or you might have a virus.

Lockups During Startup

Suppose you are starting Windows, everything looks fine, and then all of a sudden your PC freezes up and just sits there. What's the deal? Well, one of the programs or files that Windows loads at startup probably is corrupted and is causing everything to come tumbling down when it loads.

If your machine is locked up, turn off the power, wait a few seconds, and turn it back on again. Do you get the same problem again? Or this time do you see a Startup menu on a black screen offering to start in Safe mode? If you have the opportunity to start in Safe Mode, do so. (Then skip the next paragraph while the rest of the readers catch up with you.)

If it locks up every time, you need to call up the Startup menu yourself. To do so, restart the computer, and hold down the Ctrl key as it starts. The Startup menu appears. Choose Safe Mode from it.

When you start Windows in Safe Mode, you start it up minus all the special device drivers and programs. This is a troubleshooting mode, not for regular operation. In Safe Mode, you can correct whatever is causing the problem. You can tell you're in Safe Mode because the words "Safe Mode" appear in each corner of the screen, and the video mode is 640×480 and 16 colors (probably less than your normal operating mode).

Because not all the drivers are loaded in Safe Mode, you cannot do certain things there. For example, you cannot use your CD-ROM drives because the drivers for them are not loaded. However, you can run ScanDisk and the Registry Checker, and some other critical Windows utilities you'll learn about later in this section.

Safe Mode is all very well and good, but it doesn't help you determine which of the many Windows setup routines is causing your problem. To determine that, you can try stepping through the system startup one step at a time. To do so, follow these steps:

1. Restart your computer, holding down Ctrl to get the Startup menu.

2. At the Startup menu, choose Step by Step Confirmation. Every step in the Windows startup will be confirmed.

3. Press Y to let each step happen. If Windows locks up at a certain point, make a note of what driver, file, or question you just answered yes to onscreen—that's what's causing your problem.

4. Now restart again and repeat steps 1 and 2, but press N when you come to the line that caused the problem. If Windows starts normally, you now know what the problem is.

You can often tell what a driver does by looking at its path onscreen. For example, if you see something like this, it's probably a file that came with Windows:

```
C:\Windows\vnetsup.vxd
```

If the problem is a certain Windows driver loading, perhaps that driver has become corrupted. Try recopying it from the Windows CD.

On the other hand, if the path includes a folder for a particular device you added, like this, that device is probably the problem:

```
C:\pagescan\drivers\rundrvr.vxd
```

If the problem is a driver for a device you recently added to your system, perhaps it conflicts with one of the other devices on your system. If the new device came with software that runs it, try uninstalling that software using Add/Remove Programs (as described in Friday Evening's session).

Then restart to see whether that took care of the problem. If so, visit the device manufacturer's Web site to see whether an updated version of the software is available. (See "Updating Device Drivers" later in this appendix.)

Registry Errors at Startup

The Windows Registry is a configuration file that contains all your settings for Windows. If the Registry becomes damaged or corrupted, Windows might not start at all, or it might start but have serious operational problems.

Sometimes when there is a Registry error, your system detects it at startup and runs a program called the Registry Checker automatically before starting Windows. If that happens, just follow the prompts to repair the Registry and let the PC restart itself.

Other, less serious, Registry problems might not be detected at Startup but can still cause Windows to malfunction as you use it. See "Fixing Windows Problems" later in this appendix.

One way to repair the Registry is to use the System Restore feature to go back to a previous version of the Registry. This is especially good if you are having Registry problems after installing a new program. See "Using System Restore" later in this appendix for details.

Missing File Error Messages at Startup

There are two types of missing file error messages that occur at Windows startup: those that prevent Windows from starting and those that don't.

Essential Missing Files

If the missing file prevents Windows from loading, you need to fix the problem right away. Do the following:

1. Write down the complete path and name of the missing file as reported onscreen. It probably looks something like this:

   `C:\Windows\System\vnetsup.vxd`

2. Restart the system using your emergency boot disk that you created when you installed Windows. When asked whether you want CD-ROM support, choose No.

> **NOTE** The reason you have to boot from your emergency boot disk is that Windows Me does not allow you to boot to a command prompt from the hard disk. Earlier versions of Windows did.

3. At the command prompt (A:\,) type **C:** and press Enter.

4. Type **CD *path*** , where *path* is the path to the missing file, and press Enter. For example:

   CD \Windows\System

5. Type **DIR *file*** and press Enter, where *file* is the name of the missing file. For example:

   DIR vnetsup.vxd

6. A list of files with that name in that folder appears. Does the missing file appear on the list?

If the missing file does not appear, find someone who has the same version of Windows as your own. Copy the needed file onto a floppy, and then copy it from the floppy to your own PC in the folder specified.

Here's how to copy the file to your PC from someone else's:

1. On the working PC, locate the file using Windows Explorer or My Computer.

2. Place a floppy disk in the drive. Then right-click the file and choose Send To, 3 1/2 Floppy.

3. Wait for the file to be copied there. Then take the disk to the non-working PC, which you have already started using the emergency boot disk.

4. Replace the emergency boot disk with the floppy containing the needed file.

5. Type **COPY A:***file* **C:***path* and press Enter, where *file* is the name of the file and *path* is the path where it goes. For example:

   COPY a:\vnetsup.vxd C:\windows\system

6. Restart your PC and cross your fingers that the copied file allows your system to start.

At the minimum, you should not get the same missing file error message again. However, you might get a different missing file message! If so, repeat the procedure to replace the other missing file(s).

If you don't have access to another computer running your version of Windows, or if the previous steps don't solve your problem, try reinstalling Windows to see whether that fixes the problem. To do so, start the system using your emergency boot disk, but choose Yes to the CD-ROM support question. Then run the Setup.exe program from your Windows Me CD-ROM.

Non-Essential Missing Files

If you see a message that a file is missing, you might be able to press Enter to continue loading Windows. If this happens, the missing file is not a critical one. You can ignore that message without harming your system, or you can attempt a fix.

You might be able to tell from looking at the file name and path whether the file is needed. For example, suppose the missing file is reported as this:

```
C :\pagescan\scanauto.dll
```

You know that PageScan was a program that ran your old scanner, which you have not had hooked up in several months. From that, you can deduct that the missing file is the driver for the scanner. That file is *supposed* to be missing—the error is that Windows still tries to load it. See "Controlling Which Programs Load at Startup" in the Saturday Evening session to prevent Windows from trying to load that file.

On the other hand, if you still use that device on your system, you want to restore the missing file. There might already be a copy on your system. Do the following to find out:

1. Press Enter to bypass the error message and continue loading Windows.

2. After Windows loads, choose Start, Search, For Files or Folders.

3. Open the Look In drop-down list and choose your hard disk (usually C) or if you have more than one hard disk, choose All Local Drives.

4. Type the missing file's name in the Search for Files or Folders Named box.

5. Click Search Now. It searches for the file on your system. A list of found files appears, as shown in Figure A.1.

Figure A.1

Find a missing file elsewhere on your hard disk, and copy it to where Windows is expecting it to be.

If you find a copy of the missing file on your hard disk, do the following:

1. If more than one version of the file appears, look at the Modified column to determine which is the most recent copy.

2. Copy that file to the folder in which Windows is expecting the file. To do this, right-click the file and choose Copy; then display the destination folder and choose Edit, Paste.

3. Restart Windows to see whether the error message still appears.

If you don't find a copy, you need to reinstall the drivers for that device. Dig up the disks that came with the device and run its Setup program. See "Updating Device Drivers" later in this appendix for details.

Fixing Windows Problems

Perhaps Windows starts up okay, but then the problems begin. Programs don't start (more than one program, that is—otherwise suspect the individual program as the problem). Or everything locks up after running a few minutes. Or error messages abound. Windows itself is probably screwed up somehow, and the problem is probably centered around invalid or conflicting entries in the Registry.

NOTE   If your PC locks up after a few minutes of activity regardless of what program you are running (or even when you aren't running any programs at all), the problem could be overheating. Make sure your processor fan is connected and working properly. Ask a techie friend to help if needed. A virus can also cause a computer to lock up unexpectedly and frequently.

In earlier versions of Windows, such problems were thorny to troubleshoot. Windows Me's new System Restore feature, however, makes the process much easier by allowing you to return to earlier versions of the Windows Registry that were saved before the problem asserted itself.

Using System Restore

Windows looks and acts the way it does because of the settings in your Registry. The Registry is really two separate files: system.dat and user.dat. System.dat maintains system settings, and user.dat maintains your individual user preferences.

System Restore automatically backs up a copy of the Registry each day, and stores the copies on your hard disk. You can also create your own restore points along the way. Then if you ever get into trouble with the system acting strangely (perhaps because of some program you've installed), you can revert to an earlier version of the Registry and—99 times out of 100—fix the problem.

For example, suppose I'm getting ready to install a new piece of shareware, but I'm not sure about its origin or quality. I can create a restore point called "Before Shareware." Then after I install the program, if my system starts acting up, I can simply revert to the Before Shareware configuration and remove any recollection from Windows of that program ever having been installed.

System Restore does not touch any data files that you have created. For example, if you install Word and create a document, and then use System Restore to restore the system to a point before Word was installed, the document will still exist unharmed on your hard disk.

Creating a Restore Point

If you're planning ahead, you can create a restore point before performing a questionable activity. Here's how:

1. Choose Start, Programs, Accessories, System Tools, System Restore. The System Restore program opens. See Figure A.2.

2. Choose Create a Restore Point, and then click Next.

3. Type a description for the restore point (such as **Before Shareware**). Then click Next.

4. Wait for the system files to be saved, and then click OK. System Restore closes and you are done.

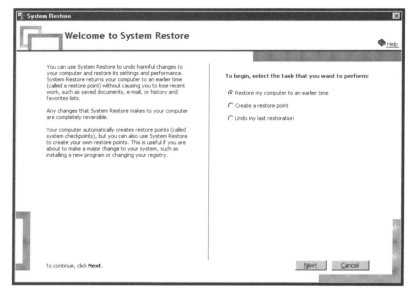

Figure A.2

The opening screen
of System Restore

Restoring to a Previous Configuration

If you are experiencing Windows problems, think back—when did the problem start? Then restore your system to a configuration prior to that date. System Restore maintains about two weeks' worth of automatic restore points, depending on the amount of available hard disk space and on your settings.

To restore a previous configuration:

1. Choose Start, Programs, Accessories, System Tools, System Restore. The System Restore program opens. See Figure A.2.

2. Choose Restore my computer to an earlier time and then click Next.

3. Choose from the calendar the date to which you want to restore.

4. Choose the restore point from that date in the box to the right of the calendar. See Figure A.3. Some dates have more than one restore point.

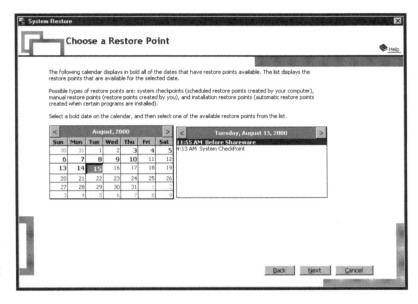

Figure A.3

Choose the date and the restore point from that date.

5. Click Next. A dialog box appears warning you not to make any changes while the restore is taking place.

6. Click OK.

7. Click Next and wait for the program to restore your system and restart it.

8. When the computer restarts, System Restore reopens automatically. Click OK to close it.

If the system works better now, great! If not, you can try a different restore point, or you can undo your last restoration.

Undoing a Restoration

All system restores are completely reversible. When you undo a restoration, you return the system to the last configuration before you restored.

To undo a restoration:

1. Choose Start, Programs, Accessories, System Tools, System Restore. The System Restore program opens. See Figure A.2.

2. Choose Undo my last restoration and click Next.

3. A confirmation box appears; click OK.

4. Click Next and wait for the restoration to be reversed and your system to restart.

5. When the system restarts, click OK to exit System Restore.

Other Possible Fixes for Windows Problems

If System Restore doesn't solve your problem, you have a choice. You can try reinstalling Windows, which takes a long time (30 minutes or more) but will probably take care of your problem, or you can fool around with some of the Windows configuration settings hoping to hit upon what ails you.

If you want to try some configuration tweaks, run MSCONFIG using the Start, Run command. You can also get to this same utility by going to System Information (Start, Programs, Accessories, System Tools, System Information) and choosing System Configuration Utility from the Tools menu there.

The System Configuration Utility, shown in Figure A.4, contains a multitude of technical settings. Here are just a few examples:

- On the General tab you can choose Normal, Diagnostic, or Selective startup. If you are having problems with Windows locking up as you start, Diagnostic and Selective startups can sometimes help you pinpoint the errant driver.

- If you need to extract a file from the Windows Me CD to replace a corrupt copy on your hard disk, the Extract File button on the General tab can help.

- The System.ini, Win.ini, and Static VXDs tabs contain listings of all the drivers and system files loaded at startup by those two files. You can deselect the check box next to any of the lines to disable it for troubleshooting purposes.

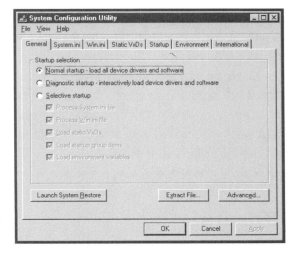

Figure A.4

The System Configuration Utility (MSCONFIG) lets you adjust Windows settings to troubleshoot problems.

✿ The Startup tab contains a listing of the programs that start automatically when Windows starts. Clear a check box next to one of them to disable it from starting (again, for troubleshooting).

A Certain Device Won't Work

If the device used to work, but no longer does, what has changed? Did you install new software? Other hardware? Did you make changes to Windows settings? Your last action before the device stopped functioning can provide a clue as to what is wrong with it.

There are five reasons why a device might not be working:

✿ It's defective.

✿ It's not installed correctly.

✿ Its drivers are not loaded.

✿ It is having a conflict with another device.

✿ There is a bug in its software or its software is not compatible with the version of Windows you have.

Defective devices need to be replaced, of course. But you can fix the other problems easily in Windows without touching the actual hardware.

NOTE If you suspect a software bug or incompatibility, visit the device manufacturer's Web site to see whether a patch or new version of the software is available. For example, as of this writing, certain scanners are incompatible under Windows Me with the motherboard in the Dell Dimension 4100 (and I happen to know this because I own one, along with one of the scanners that doesn't work with it!). I am waiting for a patch to be posted, and by the time you read this, I will probably have solved the problem by downloading a fix either from the scanner manufacturer or from Dell.

Updating Device Drivers

If a device no longer works after upgrading from an earlier version of Windows to Windows Me, you probably need an updated driver for the device. A *driver* is a file that helps Windows interact with a piece of hardware. Windows Me comes with drivers for some of the most popular devices, and most new devices also come with drivers on a disk for use in Windows.

Device drivers can come from any of several sources, including:

⚙ Windows Me provides drivers for many common devices on its own CD.

⚙ Most devices come with a disk containing drivers for various operating systems, including Windows Me. If the device has no driver specifically for Windows Me, but it does have one for Windows 98, that driver will usually work.

⚙ Many device manufacturers provide updated drivers on their Web sites.

What to do first? It's a judgment call. If you think you have the needed driver on disk, continue on to the following steps to try to update the driver. Or, if you are pretty sure you don't have it, skip ahead to the section "Downloading Drivers from the Web."

Ready to update the driver for a device? Follow these steps:

1. Right-click My Computer and choose Properties.

2. Click the Device Manager tab.

3. Locate the device for which you want to update the driver. (Click a plus sign to expand a category.)

4. Double-click the device. Its Properties box appears.

5. Click the Driver tab.

6. Click the Update Driver button. An Update Driver Wizard runs. Click Next.

7. If you have a disk that came with the device, put it in your floppy or CD-ROM drive.

8. Leave Automatic search for a better driver selected, and click Next.

9. Wait for the Wizard to look at the available drivers and determine which is the best. Then click Finish to accept its recommendation and install an updated driver if needed.

    If you have downloaded a driver from the Web, it probably won't be on a CD or floppy, so you need to go a slightly different route. Complete steps 1–6 in the previous procedure, and then do the following:

10. Choose Specify the Location of the Driver and click Next.

11. Mark the Specify a Location check box.

12. Click the Browse button. Locate the folder in which the downloaded driver resides, and then click OK to return to the Wizard.

13. Click Next, and wait for the best driver to be located.

14. Click Finish to install it.

Downloading Drivers from the Web

If an error or incompatibility in the device's software is causing a problem, visit the manufacturer's Web site. Perhaps an update or patch is available that can correct the problem. For example, when I first got my scanner, the lamp inside never turned off, no matter how long it was idle. Although this was not a critical problem, I found it annoying. I downloaded a fix from the manufacturer's Web site that corrected the problem.

If you think you might benefit from downloading an update, you first must determine the Web site address. If you're lucky, the address is printed somewhere on the device's documentation. You can also try the obvious address by typing **www.**, the *company name*, and **.com**, as in http://www.microsoft.com. Finally, you can search for the company's site using a search engine such as http://www.yahoo.com. If you can't get the driver from the manufacturer, try the very helpful Web site http://www.windrivers.com.

● ●

I'm assuming that you have been through the Sunday Morning session in this book and know about using the Internet.

● ●

After you arrive at the manufacturer's home page, where are the downloads? Most sites have an obvious hyperlink such as Download or Support. Wade through until you find what you want. Then do the following:

1. Click the link for the file to download. A File Download dialog box will appear, asking what you want to do with the file.

2. Choose the default (Save this program to disk), and then click OK. A Save As dialog box appears, asking where you want to save it.

   You can save the file anywhere you like, but make sure you remember where you put it. I created a special folder on my hard disk called Downloads in which I place all downloads.

3. Select the location and click Save. Then wait for the file to be transferred to your PC.

While you are waiting you can do other work as it transfers, but do not terminate your Internet connection until the download is finished.

When the file finishes, a box appears with Open and Open Folder buttons. Click the Open button, which opens the downloaded file and starts the patch or update installation.

> **NOTE** If you open the file and nothing happens, or if you can't open the file, perhaps it is a compressed Zip archive. Windows comes with support for compressed folders but it is not installed by default. Use Add/Remove Programs to add that utility, and then you'll be able to browse the contents of a Zip file as you can a folder.

Redetecting Plug-and-Play Hardware

Sometimes if a device isn't working, all it needs is a little "shake." One way to provide that is to remove it from Device Manager and let Windows redetect it and reinstall any drivers that it needs. Here's how to do that:

1. Right-click My Computer and choose Properties.

2. Click the Device Manager tab.

3. Locate and select the device. (Click a plus sign to expand a category.)

4. Press the Delete key to delete the device.

5. Click Refresh to redetect new devices. Windows should redetect the device and reinstall it in Device Manager.

6. If Windows does not immediately redetect the device, restart Windows; it should redetect it at startup.

7. If Windows does not redetect the device at startup, run the setup software that came with the device.

Resolving Device Conflicts

If a device doesn't work after trying the preceding fix, perhaps it is having a resource conflict with another device. A *resource conflict* occurs when two devices are trying to claim the same system resources for themselves. There are three basic types of resources that devices use:

✿ **Interrupt Requests (IRQs).** These are access paths to the processor. Each device with an IRQ can interrupt the processor's main operations to say "Hey, I need something here!" IRQs are numbered 0 through 15. Generally speaking, each device should have its own IRQ. However, some devices can share without reporting any conflicts.

⚙ **Input/Output Ranges.** These are segments of the computer's memory, and each device should have its own unique reserved area.

⚙ **DMA Channels.** These are channels, similar to IRQs, that some devices use to communicate with the processor. Sound cards and floppy drives typically use DMA channels; most other devices do not. You probably will not have any DMA channel conflicts because there are normally more than enough of them to go around.

All these resources are usually assigned automatically in Windows by Plug and Play. Allowing Windows to assign resources is a good idea in most cases. But some devices can have quirks that require them to use certain addresses or IRQs; and when two devices want the same resource, a conflict occurs, causing one or both devices to malfunction or fail to function at all.

The standard way of resolving conflicts in Windows is to turn off the Plug-and-Play assignment for a device and to specify an alternative set of resources it should use.

The following steps show you how to look for and resolve a device conflict:

1. Right-click My Computer and choose Properties.

2. Click the Device Manager tab.

3. Look for a device with a yellow circle and an exclamation point next to it. This indicates a device conflict or some other problem (such as the driver not being installed).

   If you do not see any devices with the yellow circle, you probably do not have any conflicts and can skip the rest of these steps.

4. Double-click the device with the conflict. Its Properties dialog box appears.

5. Click the Resources tab.

6. Check the Conflicting device list. If a conflict is listed, note whether it is an Input/Output Range conflict or an IRQ conflict.

7. Deselect the Use automatic settings check box.

8. Open the Settings based on drop-down list and choose a new configuration. Keep trying different configurations until you find one that reports No conflicts in the Conflicting device list. See Figure A.5.

9. Click OK to close the dialog box.

10. Click Close to close the System Properties.

11. Restart the PC and try using the device.

In rare cases, all the configurations on the list (step 8) have a conflict. If you face this situation, you can try changing the Interrupt Request and the Input/Output Range separately. Keep choosing configurations until you find one with only one conflict. Make a note of what it is. Then click the matching line in the Resource Settings list. Next, click Change Setting. One of two things can happen: you might see a message that the setting cannot be modified, or you might see a dialog box containing alternative settings. If you see the latter, try a different setting. Repeat this procedure until you find a setting that produces no conflicts.

Figure A.5

In this case, configuration 0001 has no conflicts, so you can use it.

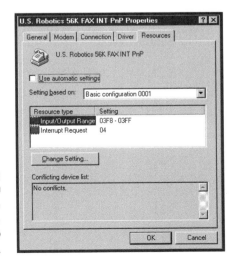

If Windows tells you that the setting cannot be modified, you have one last remedy to try. In the Conflicting device list, notice the device that is the other half of the conflict. Then try modifying the settings for that device so that it no longer conflicts with the current one.

A Certain Program Won't Run

When a program doesn't work, you probably experience one of the following symptoms; each has its own fix.

- **Nothing happens at all.** This is probably a Windows problem rather than a problem with the individual application. Restart the PC and try again. If the problem still occurs, and it happens only with this program, uninstall and reinstall the program, as described in the Friday Evening session.

- **You see an error message saying there is a missing file.** See "Non-Essential Missing Files" earlier in this appendix.

- **The program runs, but then locks up.** If it's a Windows program, uninstall and reinstall it. If it's a DOS-based program, run the MS-DOS Programs Troubleshooter in the Help system.

To get to the MS-DOS Programs Troubleshooter, do the following:

1. Choose Start, Help.

2. Enter MS-DOS in the Search box and press Enter.

3. In the list of hyperlinks that appears, click MS-DOS-based Programs Troubleshooter.

4. Work through the troubleshooter, as shown in Figure A.6, to help solve the problem.

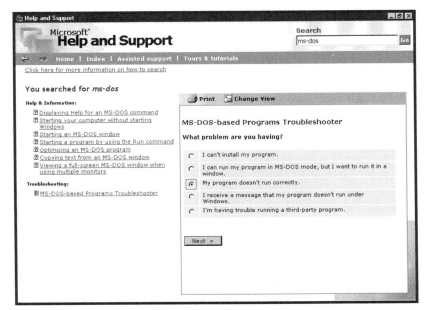

Figure A.6

Windows Help can offer suggestions for configuring MS-DOS programs.

INDEX

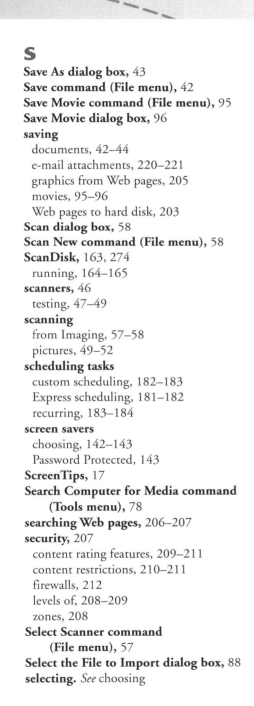

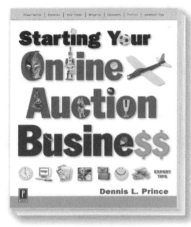
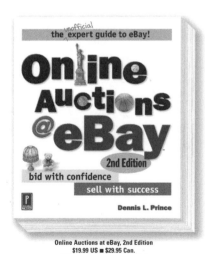